*A*FALCONGUIDE®

BASIC ESSENTIALS® SERIES

Basic Essentials®

Edible Wild Plants and Useful Herbs

Third Edition

JIM MEUNINCK

FALCO

GUILFORD, CO
HELENA, MC

AN IMPRINT OF THE GLOBE PEQUOT PRESS

FALCONGUIDE ®

Photo credits: Pages 55, 56, and 57, maples and oaks; courtesy of Fernwood Botanic Gardens. Page 61, jojoba photo: © 2006 Steven Foster. Page 62, Indian breadroot illustration: USDA-NRCS Plants Database/Britton, N. L., and A. Brown, *Illustrated Flora of the Northern States and Canada,* vol. 2 (1913). Page 77, death camas photo: Lee Casebere, USDA-NRCS Plants Database-USDA NRCS, *Northeast Wetland Flora: Field Office Guide to Plant Species* (Chester, PA: Northeast National Technical Center, 1995). Page 87, author photo: courtesy Roy Clumpner. All other photographs by Jim Meuninck.

Text design by Nancy Freeborn

Library of Congress Cataloging-in-Publication Data is available.
ISBN-13: 978-0-7627-4086-4
ISBN-10: 0-7627-4086-8

Printed in China
Third Edition/Fourth Printing

To buy books in quantity for corporate use
or incentives, call **(800) 962–0973, ext. 4551,**
or e-mail **premiums@GlobePequot.com.**

The identification, selection, and processing of any wild plant for use as food requires reasonable care and attention to details since, as indicated in the text, certain parts are wholly unsuitable for use and, in some instances, are even toxic. Because attempts to use any wild plants for food depend on various factors controllable only by the reader, the author and publisher assume no responsibility whatsoever for adverse health effects of such failures as might be encountered in the individual case. Readers are encouraged to seek medical help whenever possible. This book is no substitute for a doctor's advice.

Contents

Acknowledgments

A backroads journey from Michigan to Vancouver Island and back covers 6,000 miles and gobbles about 200 gallons of gas. My spouse, Jill, my daughter, Becca, and I have made the trip seven times. We conceived this book around a campfire on one of those crossings. Other memories persist, like the night we counted shooting stars atop the van, somewhere off a Wyoming road near a mom-and-pop diner that made the greatest blackberry shakes. I miss that, and those Montana-mountain-stream mornings when I watched Jill and Becca wash each other's hair. I long for those scary fireside stories, our old blue tent, and the chipmunk that hitched a thousand-mile ride. Let's do it again, let's take a flying leap into the "big boil" and swim the treacherous maelstrom through Firehole Canyon. C'mon Becca, let's go wiggle our toes in a wilderness hot springs and sing "B-I-N-G-O, B-I-N-G-O!" until Mom screams "Stop!"

Thanks also to my editor, mountain man Bill Schneider, who sparked this third edition, and Paula Brisco, whose hard work and precision made it worth reading. Let's all get together sometime. I know a great place, a hot springs in Idaho. We can meet Jeff Serena and the Urbans there. Bring your fly rods; it's just a 20-foot pitch from the sulphur springs to the adjacent trout stream. We can soak our bones, catch fish, count eagles, taunt bears, and spin yarns.

Introduction

Basic Essentials: Edible Wild Plants and Useful Herbs is a record of forty years of experience put to pen, experience I've gained foraging for edible and medicinal wild-flowers in the United States, Japan, China, Europe, and Canada. This record, however, is not new. Thousands—perhaps millions—of years ago, our ancestors discovered by trial and error which plants were edible and which plants were poisonous.

Today modern studies by anthropologists around the globe suggest that eating wild plants and flowers may have numerous benefits beyond good taste. Unlike many cultivars we buy in the supermarket, these plants have not been genetically manipulated or weakened by hybridization. They are vigorous and rich in the nutrients and phytochemicals our bodies need and contain essentially complete germ plasma untampered by human hands. The more than one hundred Paleolithic plants described in this book are high in fiber, calcium, and protein and full of vitamins and minerals. They are low in fat, too. Many contain healthful omega-3 essential fatty acids, which help prevent inflammatory conditions that may lead to heart disease, arthritis, and cancer.

This book is organized somewhat differently than traditional field guides. Most books are organized by season or by flower color. I have chosen to identify plants as you would stumble across them walking in a woods, trekking through a meadow, or paddling through a marsh. This practical approach begins with the familiar and progresses to the unfamiliar. All of the plants described in this book can be found in the contiguous United States, and most of the plants can also be found on my DVD and video, *Edible Wild Plants*. See appendix 3 for information on this and other recommended videos and books.

Let's begin our walk back through time along the tangled and twisted path of our ethnobotanical heritage. The trail will uncover authoritative, practical tips on gathering, preparing, and cultivating edible wild plants. You'll learn how to identify edible berries and how to make berry-delicious desserts, herbal teas, and other proven recipes from my forty years of experience and the vast human record that preceded me. Here and there along the path, modern medicinal uses will be uncovered and wildflower seed sources will be surveyed. Poisonous plants also will be attended to (see appendix 2: Poisonous Plants and Poisonous Look-alikes).

The story opens in Painter Marsh, a typical wetland harboring edible, water-loving flora.

JIM'S TOP-TEN EDIBLE WILDFLOWERS

1. Woodland violets *(Viola spp.)*
2. Bee balm *(Monarda fistulosa, M. didyma)*
3. Elder *(Sambucus canadensis, S. nigra)*
4. Wild carrot, Queen Anne's lace
   (Daucus carota)
5. Cattail *(Typha latifolia)*
6. Dandelions *(Taraxacum officinale)*
7. Mint (peppermint, spearmint, mountain mint)
   (Mentha spp.)
8. Garden sorrel *(Oxalis spp.)*
9. Hawthorn *(Crataegus spp.)*
10. Evening primrose *(Oenothera biennis)*

JIM'S TOP-TEN FAVORITE EDIBLE WILD PLANTS
In the order I prefer, by the volume I eat.

1. Dandelions *(Taraxacum officinale)*
2. Stinging nettle *(Urtica dioica)*
3. Violets *(Viola spp.)*
4. Watercress *(Nasturtium officinale)*
5. Wild leeks *(Allium tricoccum)*
6. Wild rice *(Zizania aquatica)*
7. Cattail *(Typha latifolia)*
8. Daylily *(Hemerocallis spp.)*
9. Elder *(Sambucus canadensis)*
10. Jerusalem artichoke *(Helianthus tuberosus)*

WILD PLANT FORAGING RULES

1. It's a good idea to watch a plant through its growth cycle before eating it. This is helpful because many wild plants taste best just as they break through the ground, when they are small, furled, and difficult to identify. By watching them grow for a year, you will know what you are looking for and where to find it.

2. Before eating any wild plants, study with an expert or take the plant to an expert for positive identification. Always cross-reference with two or more field guides. Make certain you have seen color photos of the plants; black-and-white photos or illustrations are not sufficient for positive identification.

3. After positive identification of an edible plant, taste only a very small amount of it. This precaution may protect you from an allergic reaction or ill effects caused by misidentification.

4. Beware of the carrot family: Hemlock, water hemlock, and other members of this family are extremely poisonous. Learn to distinguish hemlock and water hemlock from elder (elderberries).

5. I do not endorse herbal medication, self-diagnosis, or self-medication. The medicinal references in this book are descriptions from what I have read. Please do not self-medicate. Consult with your physician.

6. Practice conservation. Never collect more plants than you intend to use. Do not pick rare or endangered species. Work with a professional botanist to restore wild plants from areas where they have disappeared. Do not plant alien or invasive species in your garden—check with your state's cooperative extension services for details.

7. Avoid harvesting plants from polluted ground. Plants growing along roads may be tainted with benzene, lead, oil, and other auto pollutants. Plants dwelling in streams and along fields near farms may be polluted with herbicides and pesticides. Forage carefully. Droppings from wild game may spread bacteria, viruses, worms, giardia, amoebas, and other forms of contamination into water nurturing wild edible plants. Be careful! Wash and cook all plants foraged from wildlands.

8. Purchase wild plants from seed and live plant purveyors like Richter's (see appendix 3). Grow them in your garden, close to your kitchen. Make wild foods an integral part of your diet.

CHAPTER ONE

Rivers, Lakes, Ponds, and Swamps

CATTAIL (*Typha latifolia*)

Description. Long, sword-shaped leaves; green flowers on tandem spikes; lower spike female, upper spike male. Worldwide range. There are two species of cattails common to North America: broad leafed and narrow leafed.

Location. Entire United States, except extreme desert climates.

WARNING. *Before eating cattail shoots, learn to distinguish young shoots from their poisonous look-alike, iris shoots (see blue flag iris in appendix 2). Cattail shoots are more round; iris shoots are flat and hard. Cattail shoots are more widely spaced, while iris shoots grow in tight clusters. If you are not certain, remember Wild Plant Foraging Rule #1.*

Cooking tips. Cattails are a versatile foodstuff. The roots, new shoots, and flowering heads are all edible. In the spring simply find the shoots, reach down into the mud, and pull. Peel off the outer leaves, and underneath is the tender tongue of cattail. Sauté this delicate core in butter for 3 to 5 minutes. Season with a few drops of soy sauce and a pinch of wild ginger.

The male flowering head (located above the female flower spike) is simple to harvest, nutritious, and freezes well. Simply strip it into a plastic bag. This high-protein flour extender will keep in your freezer for eight months. Freeze the pollen, stamens, and anthers for year-round use in baked goods.

The young female bloom spike can be cooked like corn on the cob. Simply boil or steam the spike in lightly salted water. Cook until tender, but-ter, and eat hot. Young spikes can be eaten uncooked. Mix five parts cattail pollen with one part honey for a quick-to-prepare high-energy food.

A bit deeper in the soil is the long root. The root core is an excellent source of starch. Eat the starch raw as quick-energy food or, better yet, crush the roots in cold water and leach out the starch. The starch can be added to soups and stews as a thickener.

Medicinal uses. Without endorsing herbal medicine, I've discovered that cattail parts have been used to treat gonorrhea, worms, and diarrhea. The chopped root is also applied to burns and minor cuts. The Chinese use the plant to stop bleeding.

PALEOLITHIC WAFFLES

In a large bowl combine the following ingredients:

½ cup low-fat Bisquick
1 cup buckwheat flour
½ cup cattail pollen or male flowering parts
1 handful of chopped walnuts
3 tablespoons ground flax seeds (best ground in a coffee mill)
⅓ cup cooked wild rice (optional)
⅓ cup cooked 12- or 20-grain cereal (optional)
½ cup blueberries and/or raspberries

Next, break in 1 egg white, pour in enough skim milk to moisten, and squeeze in the juice of half a lemon. Spray waffle iron with canola spray, pour in waffle mix, and pre-pare to enjoy one of the most sustaining, high-fiber, energy-rich, and protein-rich breakfasts you will ever have. Makes five waffles.

WATERCRESS (*Nasturtium officinale*)

Description. Grows along the margins of shallow, clean water. Alternate leaves to ¾ inch in width, ovate, simple, broad near base; small white flower with four petals. To avoid contamination from pesticides and herbicides, collect watercress (and, for that matter, all edible water plants) from a clean water source such as a highland stream or free-flowing spring.

Watercress is a pungent, spicy green. It's an important ingredient in V8 vegetable juice and one of the most useful greens known to humankind. In the northern United States and Canada, watercress is available ten months a year. South of the Mason-Dixon Line, it's a year-round food. Watercress is high in vitamins C and A.

Location. Throughout the United States.

WARNING. *It's a good idea to cook all watercress gathered from the bush to avoid possible contamination with giardia and other waterborne parasites and contaminants.*

Cooking tips. Scramble chopped watercress with eggs, stuff a pita sandwich, add it to salads, or make watercress soup. I like to stir-fry watercress with 1 tablespoon of olive oil, 2 tablespoons of soy sauce, 1 tablespoon of lemon juice, 1 teaspoon of diced ginger root, and the juice of 1 pressed garlic clove. Cook briefly at medium heat for about 2 minutes. Your can also use watercress as a stuffing when preparing smoked or baked bass. After washing the body cavity, stuff the fish with watercress, season to taste, and bake or smoke it.

Medicinal uses. Mild diuretic. A few Indian groups used watercress to dissolve gallstones.

DUCKWEED (*Lemna* spp.)

Description. Floating plant; one or two ³⁄₁₆-inch oval leaves; threadlike root hairs.

You've probably seen duckweed—it's the green slime completely covering ponds, backwaters, and sloughs in midsummer. Upon closer inspection, the green water cover is one of the smallest flowering plants. This plant is hydroponic; the tiny root hairs siphon nutrients from the water.

Location. Found nationwide.

WARNING. *Use this plant sparingly, as you would all wild plants. If you have any food allergies, be especially careful.*

Cooking tips. Duckweed is edible. Intrepid foragers can blend it into their favorite soup recipe. More conservative folks use it sparingly, as duckweed has an unusual, tough texture that is pleasing to some and distasteful to others.

Medicinal uses. The Chinese use duckweed to treat hypothermia, flatulence, and acute kidney infections.

REED GRASS (*Phragmites communis*)

Description. Tall wetland grass; lance-shaped leaves up to 1 foot in length; flowers in tall, dense plume. Plants grow in dense cluster. Reed grass is found around the margins of streams and in wet lowlands. The root of reed grass, like cattail roots, can be harvested and leached of its starch. *Note:* The dried, hollow stalks of reed can be cut to 4-inch lengths and used as spigots for tapping maple trees for syrup.

Location. Throughout the United States.

Cooking tips. The first shoots of spring can be eaten raw but are best steamed until tender. Prepare the plant immediately after picking, as delays in preparation make for a tough, stringy meal. Simply chop the new shoots into a manageable size and place them in a steamer. They are ready to eat in 5 minutes. In the fall, seeds can be ground into flour or stripped, crushed, and cooked with berries. Also try reed seeds cooked in stews and soups.

Medicinal uses. The Chinese use this plant to clear fevers, quench thirst, promote diuresis, and promote salivation.

WILD RICE (*Zizania aquatica*)

Description. Tall reedlike grass; long, narrow leaf blades; flowers in tall plume; upper flowers female, lower flowers male. Wild rice is a tall grass found growing in shallow, clean water. The seeds can be harvested in August and September. Timing is critical, so check your stand of wild rice often. Mature seeds drop off easily.

Return every other day to maximize the harvest.

Use a rolling pin to thresh the husks from the seed. Simply roll back and forth over the grain. Use a fan or the wind to dispel the chaff.

Location. Eastern United States, roughly to the Mississippi River.

Cooking tips. The simplest way to cook wild rice is to boil 2 cups of lightly salted water, add 1 cup of wild rice, and cover and simmer for 35 minutes. Makes an excellent stuffing for wild turkey. Wild rice, cooked until tender, is an excellent addition to pancake and waffle mixes. It also goes well in twelve- and twenty-grain hot cereals and is a great substitute for white rice. Extend your supply by cooking it half and half with long-grain brown rice.

YELLOW POND LILY, SPATTERDOCK
(*Nuphar variegatum, N. luteum*)

Description. These two closely related species are found in ponds, shallow lakes, and streams. Their disk-shaped leaves unfurl above water. The yellow flower blooms through the summer and bears a primitive-looking fruit. The fruit pod contains numerous seeds—perhaps the only palatable part of this plant. The root stock of spatterdock can be cut free and boiled. It smells sweet like an apple, but it's a bitter pill to swallow—even after cooking in two or three changes of water. Strictly a survival food, when nothing else is available.

Location. Throughout the United States, except extreme mountain and desert regions.

N. luteum

Cooking tips. The seeds can be dried and ground into flour or prepared like popcorn. Place the dried seeds in a popcorn popper. Cover the machine so the small seeds don't become airborne. The results are usually disappointing. Seeds simply pop open, but they're edible with salt and butter.

Medicinal uses. Root poulticed on wounds, swellings, boils, and inflamations. Root tea used to treat chills and fever.

FRAGRANT WATER LILY
(*Nymphaea odorata*)

Description. Large, platter-shaped leaves that float flat, 6 to 10 inches in diameter; large white flower. The fragrant water lily is edible and is also simple to transplant. Simply place it in a clay pot submerged in fresh water.

Location. Eastern United States, roughly to the Mississippi.

Cooking tips. Pioneers ate the unfurled leaves and the unopened flower buds. The flower petals can be eaten with salad greens.

Medicinal uses. Dried root used to treat mouth sores and as an astringent.

ARROWHEAD, WAPATO
(*Sagittaria latifolia*)

Description. Arrow-shaped leaves, veins palmate; white flower, three platter-shaped petals. Arrowhead (also called wapato) has an edible tuber attached to its root.

Location. Found from Maine to Washington down through California.

WARNING. *Arrowhead looks similar to the poisonous arrow arum (see appendix 2). To avoid confusing the two, note that* arrowhead leaves are palmate (all veins run out from a single source like fingers on the palm of a hand), whereas arrow arum has pinnate veins (veins that run out along the entire length of the midrib vein that dissects the leaf). Best to follow this plant through one year's growth cycle to avoid confusion.

Cooking tips. The arrowhead tuber can be harvested in the fall, winter, or spring. Boil the tuber until tender. Remove the peel, mash the contents in a frying pan, and cook like hash browns.

Medicinal uses. Native Americans used the root to treat tuberculosis. Root used internally to treat fever.

PICKERELWEED
(*Pontederia cordata*)

Description. Arrow-shaped leaf, veins spread from base, merge at tip like venation in grass leaves; blue flowers, densely clustered spikes. Young leaves and mature seeds can be eaten. Leaves most tender in spring, while unfurling beneath water.

Location. Entire United States, except extreme desert, southern California, and lower Florida.

Cooking tips. Cook leaves with dandelions and mustard greens. Season cooked greens with Italian dressing and serve hot. Add flower petals to salads. In late summer, seeds mature in tough, leathery capsules. Open capsule to get fruit. Munch as a trail food or dry and grind into flour.

WILD ROSE (*Rosa* spp.)

Description. Bush; spiny branches; white, pink, or red flowers; leaves alternate, compound, sharply toothed margins. Common edible flower found along the margins of waterways. Plant's autumn flowers give rise to the famous fruit, the rose hip.

Location. Various species found throughout the United States, except extreme desert regions.

Cooking tips. Petals are sweet and aromatic. Rose petals and leaves can be dried and used for tea. Add to summer floral salads. Rose water can be made by boiling aromatic rose petals in a still made with an Erlenmeyer flask, rubber stopper, copper coil, and collecting jar. Using rose water as a marinade for skinless chicken adds both flavor and aroma.

Medicinal uses. An excellent source of vitamin C, rose hips are used to prevent scurvy. The Chinese and Native Americans used rose tea to treat worms and intestinal disorders.

AMERICAN ELDER, ELDERBERRY
(*Sambucus canadensis, S. cerulea, S. racemosa, S. nigra*)

Description. Shrub; featherlike leaf, compound, leaflet number variable, ten to twelve leaflets typical, toothed; white flowers in dense, flat, or rounded cluster; blue to black to red berries. American elder thrives along the edges of streams, bogs, and other wetlands. *S. canadensis* has black berries. *S. cerulea* has blue berries. Two subspecies of *S. racemosa,* black elder and red elder, have black to purple and red berries, respectively.

Location. *S. canadensis* is found in the eastern United States, roughly to the Mississippi. *S. cerulea* and *S. racemosa* are found in the western United States.

WARNING. *Learn to distinguish elder flowers from poisonous water hemlock flowers (see appendix 2). Cross-reference with two or three field guides, and forage with a knowledgeable botanist. Make positive, expert identification. Make certain you have seen color photos of the two plants. Also, always cook red elderberries, as the raw berries may cause you to vomit.*

S. canadensis

Cooking tips. Elderberries mature in late summer and can be boiled into fruit drink, made into jelly, or fermented into wine. Elderberries later in the year can be dried in a food drier or simply frozen fresh. Dried elderberries can be stirred into bread, waffle, pancake, and cookie mixes. You can eat the flower heads raw or make a rice-flour dip and deep-fry them. You can make elder flower brandy by mixing the same amount of brandy by volume with the same amount of flowers by weight— for example 5 ounces of brandy with 5 ounces of flowers. Make certain to strip flowers off the cluster and into the brandy and keep elderberry stems out of the brew. Let the mix sit (refrigerated) for two weeks, then strain it through cheese-cloth or nylon panty hose and enjoy. Try this recipe with port or sherry, too.

Medicinal uses. Elderberry extracts are antiviral. In Europe elderberry syrup (Sam-bucol) is used to prevent and treat colds and flu. Elder flowers contain rutin and quercetin, bioflavonoids useful in preventing heart disease. Antioxidant rich, the flowers also provide protection from cancer-causing free-radical damage.

ELDERBERRY-APPLE PIE

2 cups elderberries
1 cup blackberries or wild grapes (without seeds)
2 cups cooking apples
3 tablespoons brown sugar, or substitute maple syrup
1 teaspoon cinnamon
½ teaspoon nutmeg
1 egg
1 teaspoon flour
3 tablespoons butter
9-inch store-bought pie shell

In a bowl mix berries and apples, then stir in brown sugar or maple syrup. Add cin-namon, nutmeg, and egg. Pour contents in layers into a 9-inch pie shell. Sprinkle a pinch of flour over each layer. Place butter over the filling. Bake pie (topless or cover with a crust) at 325°F for 45 minutes.

CHAPTER TWO

North American Berries

MOUNTAIN ASH (*Sorbus sitchensis, S. americana, S. decora*)

Description. Shrub or small tree to 40 feet. Compound leaves, eleven to seventeen toothed leaflets; leaves long and narrow, three times longer than broad; flowers and fruit in rounded clusters. Berries are red when ripe, best after a frost.

Location. S. *sitchensis* is found in the western United States; S. *americana* northern tier of the eastern states.

Cooking tips. Berries are best after a frost (or you can freeze and thaw them in the freezer). Their high pectin content makes them a good addition to preserves and jellies. Mix about ¼ cup mountain ash berries to 1 cup blueberries or cherries. Boiled berries may be used as relish for meat, sweeten to taste. Green or ripe fruit may be mashed and used to marinate meat.

Medicinal uses. Native Americans used the inner bark and gummy terminal buds of S. *americana* as a tonic. The tonic is reported to enhance mood and treat depression. Bark and bud infusion is considered antimicrobial and an appetite stimulant. Inner bark and/or gummy red terminal buds are infused for colds. Inner

S. decora

bark infusion used to reduce pain after childbirth; root infusion used to treat colic. Root and bark decoction used for treating rheumatism and arthritis. Wood ash is styptic and considered useful for treating burns and boils. Root of sweet flag and *S. americana* were combined and infused as spring tonic. Berries used as a digestive aid. Twigs of western species used as chewing stick (toothbrush).

AUTUMN OLIVE
(*Elaeagnus umbellata*)

Description. Bush or shrub to 18 feet. Long, ovate leaves, toothless and leathery, width less than half the length, length usually between ¾ and 1½ inches; leaves silvery underneath. Leaves, twigs, and berries are speckled; yellow white flowers cluster in leaf axils. Scarlet speckled berries about the size of a currant. Ripens in September.

Location. Edges of woods and fence rows, in meadows, throughout the eastern United States and southern Canada.

Cooking tips. Eat out of hand. Simmer berries to juice, then strain away seeds with a food mill or sieve. Use this reduced sauce over pancakes, waffles, wontons, and egg rolls. Jam recipe: 8 cups berries mixed with ½ cup agar flakes. Bring to a boil in a pan, stirring continuously. Lower heat, cover, simmer for 15 minutes, stirring occasionally. Strain seeds and use as a freezer jam.

Medicinal use. Antiscorbutic: Vitamin C content prevents scurvy.

EVERGREEN HUCKLEBERRY
(*Vaccinium ovatum*)

Description. Bushy evergreen shrub to 7 feet. Twigs hairy, reddish in color; leaves evergreen, finely toothed, ½ to 1 inch long, oval, thick, waxy; bell-shaped pink flowers. Blooms May to July depending on altitude and weather. Small, sweet, shiny black berries. Favorite bear food.

Location. Typically West Coast and mountain states from Alaska to California.

Cooking tips. Eat out of hand or in hot and cold cereals or use to make jam. Marinade recipe. Simmer 1 cup berries, stir in 1 teaspoon Dijon mustard, 1 tablespoon soy sauce, 1 tablespoon crushed ginger, and the juice of half a lemon. Use marinade on salmon and chicken or as dip for wontons.

Medicinal uses. High in antioxidants, including anthocyanin. For diabetics these berries may help manage blood-sugar levels.

STRAWBERRY (*Fragaria virginiana, F. vesca, F. californica*)

Description. White flower; sharply toothed leaflets in threes. Wild strawberries are found in meadows and open woods. Harvest in late May and early June. Strawberries are high in vitamin C and are fiber rich—a good choice for dieters.

F. virginiana

Location. F. virginiana is found in the eastern United States, roughly to the Mississippi; F. vesca is found west of the Mississippi River; and F. californica is found in California and Baja.

Medicinal uses. Native Americans used strawberries to treat gout, scurvy, and kidney infections. Root tannins were used to treat malaria. The fruits contain ellagic acid.

R. idaeus

RASPBERRY (*Rubus idaeus, R. occidentalis*)

Description. Shrub; spiny branches; compound leaves, three to five leaflets, sharply toothed; white flowers, three or more petals. Red and black raspberries are found along the fringes of woods, fencerows, and the margins of fields. Berries are ready for harvest in late spring and early summer.

Location. Throughout the United States.

Cooking tips. Use as pie filling or stir into pancake batter and muffin mixes. Makes excellent jam or jelly.

Medicinal uses. Leaves can be steeped in tea and used as a tonic for pregnant women. Native Americans used root for diarrhea and dysentery. Also used to flavor medicines. Like other berries, it's a great dietary choice for weight watchers. High in cancer-fighting ellagic acid. One cup of raspberries per day shows promise as an anticancer agent. Nananone, the frosty appearance of wild raspberries, is an antifungal agent that protects the berries from fungal infections. That's why wild raspberries do not spoil as quickly as cultivars that have lost their capacity to produce nananone.

BERRY GOOD MUFFINS

Here's all the energy you need to kick off the day.

1 whole seedless orange
1 cup strawberries or raspberries
1 cup blackberries or mulberries (or any other berries, including rose hips)
1 egg
½ cup vegetable oil
1½ cups flour
¾ cup sugar
1 teaspoon baking powder
1 teaspoon baking soda
1 teaspoon salt
½ cup raisins
1 cup black walnuts

Combine orange—peel and all—with all berries. Add egg and vegetable oil. Blend. Mix flour, sugar, baking powder, baking soda, and salt. Add raisins and walnuts. Bake at 375°F for 20 minutes. Makes six muffins.

BLACKBERRY (*Rubus allegheniensis, R. laciniatus*)

Description. Similar to raspberry. Shrub; spiny branches; compound leaves, 5+/- leaflets, toothed; white flower bloom appears after raspberries. *R. laciniatus* has sharply cut leaves. Blackberries are often found near your raspberry source. There are several species. Blackberries ripen in mid- and late summer.

R. allegheniensis

Location. Throughout the United States.

Cooking tips. Here's a low-calorie, high-nutrition breakfast made with raspberries, blackberries, or both. Mix 2 cups berries with 2 cups low-fat sweetened vanilla yogurt. Add a dash of milk and blend—a wonderful ice-cream substitute with half the sugar and fat. Also use in pies, muffins, pancakes, jellies, and jams. Make tea from the leaves.

Medicinal uses. Native Americans used roots with other herbs for eye sores, back-aches, and stomachaches. Pioneers made blackberry vinegar to treat gout and arthritis. The Chinese use *Rubus* species in a tea to stimulate circulation—they claim it helps alleviate pain in muscles and bones. Blackberries also contain several cancer-fighting antioxidants.

BLUEBERRY (*Vaccinium* spp.)

Description. Shrub; leaves alternate, simple, smooth margin; flowers white to pink, tightly clustered. Blueberries are available from early summer through early autumn. There are several species. Found in high-lands, lowlands, openlands, and wooded areas.

Location. Various species found throughout the United States.

Cooking tips. For a simple blueberry treat, pour a bowl of frozen blueberries and cover them with half-and-half, whole milk, or low-fat milk. This frozen dessert sets up quickly and is ready to eat—a refreshing, cooling, low-sugar, world-class treat. Use blueberries in pies, pancakes, and other fruit recipes described in this book.

Medicinal uses. Blueberries contain anthocyanin that may protect you from *E. coli* infections. This is a fine bioflavonoid-rich food that protects you from degenerative disease. Native Americans used the antioxidant qualities of blueberries to preserve foods such as pemmican.

GOOSEBERRY AND CURRANT (*Ribes* spp.)

Description. Shrub; spiny branches; gooseberry fruit is spined, while currant has smooth or spined fruit; deeply lobed leaves, sharply toothed; flowers yellow, purplish, or white (depending on species). You can find gooseberries and currants in woodlands and along the margins of woods. There are several species. The spiny, dangerous-looking berries are harmless and ready for harvest in early summer.

Gooseberry

Location. Various species found throughout the United States.

Cooking tips. Make Gooseberry-Currant Pie from the Elderberry-Apple Pie recipe (see page 9). Be certain to add lemon juice to punch up the taste.

Medicinal uses. Gooseberries and currants are made into a jelly spiced with peppermint, lemon juice, and ginger, then taken as a sore throat remedy. Others claim that gamma-linolenic acid (GLA), an active ingredient of currants, may prevent acne, obesity, and schizophrenia.

MULBERRY (*Morus* spp.)

Description. Small to medium-size tree; leaves simple, alternate, toothed, round or slightly elongated, broadest near base; flowers green, tiny, clustered on spike. Not far from gooseberries are mulberries. Mulberry trees are found along roads, the fringes of woods, fencerows, and about anywhere berry-eating birds have redistributed the

seeds. There are red, white, and black varieties. Ripened fruits are very edible.

Location. Eastern United States, roughly to the Mississippi.

WARNING. *Do not eat the unripened fruits and leaves because they are slightly hallucinogenic.*

Cooking tips. Mulberries, gooseberries, and currants can be combined or used separately to make fudge.

Medicinal uses. White mulberry *(M. alba)* leaf extraction has shown promise as a treatment for elephantiasis. The fruits of both white and red mulberry *(M. rubra)* are said to reduce fever.

Botanists say mulberry leaves and unripened fruits have a mild sedative effect. Ripe fruit cooked with sugar and mixed with vodka has a stimulating effect.

MULBERRY FUDGE

This candy has a taffylike consistency and is messy to eat. Gooseberries and currants, in combination or separately, can also be used.

1 pound mulberries
½ cup water
2 cups sugar
5 tablespoons butter

Gently cook mulberries in ½ cup water until hot, then mash berries through a fine sieve to separate the juice. Add sugar to mashed berries. Add butter, then reheat slowly to dissolve butter. Bring to a boil over medium heat. Do not stir. Let mix form a hot, soft ball. (This will occur at between 235°F and 240°F on a candy thermometer.) Cool until warm, then whip the mixture with a wooden spoon for a few seconds. Press the mixture into a buttered 9-inch pie pan and cut into pieces. Eat immediately or cover and refrigerate.

WILD GRAPE (*Vitis* spp.)

Description. Climbing vine; clinging tendrils; green flowers in a large cluster; leaves alternate, simple, round, toothed, with heart-shaped base. The young leaves and ripe fruits are edible. They are found clinging to and climbing trees, walls, and fences.

Location. Eastern United States, roughly to the Mississippi.

WARNING. *The Canadian moonseed plant looks like wild grape but is poisonous. Learn to distinguish these two plants before eating what you think are wild grapes. Get expert identification.*

Cooking tips. To make raisins, cover wild grapes with cheesecloth and dry them in the sun for three days, or dry them in a food dryer. Grape leaves can be wrapped around rice, vegetables, and meat and steamed until tender. Add grape leaves to pickling spices when preparing dill pickles.

Medicinal uses. The fruit, leaves, and tendrils have been used by Native Americans and pioneers to treat hepatitis, diarrhea, and snakebite. Native Americans used tonic made with grape and several other herbs to increase fertility. Tannins and other phenolic compounds found in grape skins may provide protection from heart disease. Resveratrol from grapes may prevent strokes and heart attacks.

STAGHORN SUMAC (*Rhus typhina*)

Description. Shrub or small tree; leaves lance shaped, alternate, compound, numerous leaflets, toothed; cone-shaped flower and berry clusters. The large berry spikes of staghorn sumac are ready to harvest in late summer.

Location. Entire United States, except extreme desert, southern California, and lower Florida.

Cooking tips. Strip red staghorn sumac berries from heads. Discard stems and heads. Soak cotton-covered berries in hot water to extract a lemonade-like drink. Steep sassafras root in the tea. Add sugar and serve.

Medicinal uses. Staghorn sumac flower can be steeped into tea and taken for stomach pain. Gargles made from berries are purported to help sore throats.

SALAL (*Gaultheria shallon*)

Description. Sprawling shrub forms dense thickets in pine forests. Oval, shiny, leathery, thick leaves are alternate, clinging to sturdy stems on petioles of varying lengths. Bell-shaped pink to white flowers are strung out like pearls near ends of stem. Dark blue to blue black fruit is ripe from July through September.

Location. Seashore west of the Cascades and coastal ranges, from California to the Alaskan peninsula.

Cooking tips. The berries can be eaten as you hike along. Take some home and blend them into jelly or maple syrup, or dry them in a food dryer and use them in muffins, waffles, and pancakes.

Medicinal uses. Native Americans chewed the leaves to stem off hunger. Dried salal berries are considered a good laxative, while the plant's dried leaves infused in water can be imbibed to treat diarrhea (the tea is astringent, thus its effectiveness). Dried leaves can also be powdered and used externally as a styptic on scrapes and abrasions. Also, dried leaf powder can be mixed with water to make a pasty poultice for wounds.

DRIED SALAL BERRY CAKES

Salal berries were an important traditional food of Native Americans of the Northwest. They gathered the berries and prepared them in cakes.

To make a fair facsimile of a dried cake, boil the berries until they are a soft mash, and then pour them into a greased cupcake pan. Fill each cupcake holder half full and bake at 200°F until the cakes are dried (about 3½ hours). The dried cakes can be reconstituted by an overnight soak in the refrigerator.

SALMONBERRY
(*Rubus spectabilis*)

Description. Shrub 6 to 7 feet in height, found along moist slopes, sunny banks, and streams. Brown stems with yellow bark, laced with weak-to-soft thorns; leaflets fuzzy with serrated edges, usually in threes, approximately 3 inches in length. Fuchsia flowers arrive with leaves in spring. Soft, dry fruit ranges from bright red to yellowish. *Note:* I find this berry on Vancouver Island along the path to Botanical Beach. To find the berries, look for bear dung.

Location. From Michigan west to the Sierras and Rockies north to Alaska.

Cooking tips. The soft (when ripe) fruit melts in your mouth and will melt in your backpack, too! Best to eat it as you hike along. Spring sprouts can be peeled, cooked, and eaten. Harvest the stems before they become hard and woody, and eat them raw, steamed, or roasted.

THIMBLEBERRY (*Rubus parviflorus*)

Description. Found in moist places (streamside, coastal). A deciduous shrub up to 7 feet high, unbarbed, erect with shredded-to-smooth bark. Large maplelike leaves, smooth or slightly hairy on top, fuzzy underneath.

Location. Mountain West, primarily the Sierras and Rockies to Alaska.

Cooking tips. Eat the soft, ripe berries in the bush. Like salmonberry (see above), thimbleberry will turn to mush in your backpack. To eat: Apply forefinger and thumb to fruit, pull and twist, and pop in your mouth. No cooking required. Try this tart berry on cereal. Northwestern Native Americans dried the berries in cakes (see page 18) or stored them in goose grease. Young shoots can be harvested, peeled, and cooked as a spring green.

Medicinal use. Native Americans (Kwakiutls of the Northwest) made a decoction, a drink for treating bloody vomiting, with boiled blackberry roots, vines, and thimbleberry.

CHAPTER THREE

Yards and Meadows

DANDELION (*Taraxacum officinale*)

Description. Flower heads yellow; leaves irregular, sharply lobed, in basal whorl; large taproot. Leaves, crown, roots, and flower petals are edible. The seeds are a favorite food of goldfinches.

Location. Throughout the United States.

Cooking tips. Dandelion leaves are high in vitamins A, C, and B1. They are best in early spring, before they flower. Bitter older leaves can be improved by soaking them for an hour or so in a bowl of water mixed with a teaspoon of baking soda.

My favorite dandelion recipe goes like this. Chop two handfuls of dandelion leaves. Mix this with ½ cup chopped nuts of your choice. Add the juice of half a lemon or lime. Blend in 3 tablespoons honey and 1 teaspoon olive oil. Mix well. Here's a meal full of vitamins and quick energy.

You can also use dandelion flowers in tossed salads. The crown of the plant— the whitish area just below the leaves and above the roots—can be deep-fried. Coat the crowns in tempura batter, then deep-fry. I pluck the flower petals and sprinkle them on any food that needs color. Here is potential cancer-fighting, Beta-carotene-rich nutrition that is free, grows everywhere, and provides for you year-round. When serving a rice dish, use dandelion petals like confetti over the rice.

From the plant's root you can make dandelion coffee. Let the root dry in a warm, dry place. Then lightly roast the root and grind it to a powder. Add 1 teaspoon of the powder to 1 cup hot water. This bitter tonic may be good for the liver.

Medicinal uses. Dandelion tea (made from roots) was used as a laxative, blood purifier, and diuretic. For 5,000 years dandelion parts have been used to clear fevers, break up congestion, and stimulate milk flow in nursing mothers. Recent evidence suggests dandelion tea may rejuvenate alcoholics' livers. Bitter root teas from dandelions, chicory, gentian, and the like may stimulate appetite and improve digestion. Plant bitters are being used experimentally to treat anorexia.

JAPANESE SAUCE

2 tablespoons soy sauce
1 tablespoon sesame seed oil
1 heaping teaspoon chopped ginger root
2 tablespoons lemon juice
1 clove garlic, diced
pinch of wasabe (Japanese hot mustard)
1 mushroom, coarsely chopped
2 cups each dandelion leaves, watercress, and stinging nettles

Combine the soy sauce, sesame seed oil, chopped ginger root, lemon, garlic, and wasabe. Stir. Add mushroom, dandelion leaves, watercress, and stinging nettles. Sauté in a wok at 375°F to 400°F for 2 to 3 minutes and serve.

CHICKWEED (*Stellaria* spp.)

Description. Leaves oval, ¼ inch to ½ inch; stem weak, hairy, prostrate, ½ inch; flower white, lance-shaped petals. A common ground cover.

Location. Eastern United States, roughly to the Mississippi.

Cooking tips. Can be eaten raw or cooked. Sprinkle chickweed flowers in with leaves when preparing a salad. A handful on a sandwich is a good substitute for alfalfa sprouts. Chopped in a stir-fry they add bulk, fiber, and a decent amount of vitamins A and C. Stew chickweed with rabbit, chicken, or beef. Add 4 cups of

flowers, leaves, and stems to a pot. Mix in favorite stewing herbs. Enter bird, bunny, or beef. Then brace yourself for a magnificent feast. Later in the year the mature seeds can be used to thicken soup. Seeds also make an excellent birdseed.

For chickweed pancakes, blanch 1 cup chickweed for 3 minutes, chop in a blender, and add blended greens to pancake batter.

Medicinal uses. Chickweed is eaten as a diuretic. Leaf tea is used as a cold-relieving expectorant.

VIOLETS (*Viola* spp.)

Description. Flower irregular; leaves vary, usually ovate; common blue violet has heart-shaped, serrated leaves. Found in shady areas along fringes of lawn. Violets are cultivated in France for perfume. This incredible edible is high in vitamins C, A, and E.

Location. Eastern United States, roughly to the Mississippi River.

WARNING. *Late-season plants without flowers can be confused with inedible greens. Forage this plant only when in bloom.*

Cooking tips. Use both the leaves and flowers in salads. Flowers can also be candied (see Candied Evening Primrose, page 53). Experiment. Put them over finished meat dishes as a garnish and color contrast that invites eating.

Medicinal uses. Violet roots consumed in large amounts are emetic and purgative. Plant used as poultice over skin abrasions. In China indigenous health care givers use one species, *V. diffusa,* to treat aplastic anemia, leukemia, mastitis, mumps, and poisonous snakebites. The violet's color suggests the presence of anthocyanin, secondary metabolites that give off a blue hue. Anthocyanin also provides protection from *E. coli* infection.

BULL THISTLE (*Cirsium vulgare*)

Description. Thorny biennial; purple flower rises from spiny bract. Barbed leaves of the first year's growth can be eaten after the spines have been stripped away with a knife. Wear gloves when harvesting roots and leaves.

Location. Eastern United States, roughly to the Mississippi.

Cooking tips. Use a knife to strip thorny armor away from leaves. Eat raw or cooked. Flavor similar to celery. Harvest leaves in the spring and fall. In summer, flower petals can be sprinkled over salads. Roots can be boiled, sliced, and stir-fried. Some folks steam outer green bract around flower heads and eat it like an artichoke.

Medicinal uses. The Chinese use thistle teas and decoctions to treat appendicitis, internal bleeding, and inflammations.

PLANTAIN, BUCKHORN (*Plantago major, P. lanceolata*)

Description. Flowers green, tiny, numerous on spike; ovate leaf with pointed tip. *Plantago major* has broad, ovate leaves; *P. lanceolata* has narrower, lancelike leaves. Plantain is best harvested before this flower stalk appears. New leaves keep coming all year.

Location. *P. lanceolata* is found in the eastern United States, roughly to the Mississippi. *P. major* is found on waste ground, roadsides, in vacant lots, and yards nationwide.

P. lanceolata

Cooking tips. Use tender young leaves in salads. Soak older leaves in diluted salt water for 10 minutes, then steam until tender. Dried seeds can be eaten whole or ground into flour.

Medicinal uses. One over-the-counter laxative uses seeds from the *psyllium* species of plantain. For more than a thousand years people have chewed plantain leaves and applied them over burns, cuts, and scrapes. In China indigenous health care givers use whole plant as tea to clear fever and promote healing.

LAMB'S-QUARTERS
(*Chenopodium album*)

Description. Lamb's-quarters (various herbs of the goosefoot family) can be found in fields, on waste ground, and in just about everyone's garden. A healthy lamb's-quarters plant can climb 3 feet tall, with leaves the shape of a lamb's hind quarter.

Location. Eastern United States, roughly to the Mississippi, and more rarely in the western United States.

Cooking tips. As a potherb, boil lamb's-quarters for 5 minutes with mustard greens and dandelion leaves. For a nutritious snack add seeds to your favorite bread or muffin mix. The young tender leaves and tips produce the best salad greens.

Medicinal uses. Native Americans used a decoration of leaves to treat arthritis. Leaves and stems cooked with beans may relieve flatulence. A wash of leaves applied to nursing mother's breast as a lactogogue may induce the flow of milk.

GILL-OVER-GROUND, GROUND IVY
(*Glechoma hederacea*)

Description. Creeping plant; purple stems; roundish, lobed, violet flowers in whorls. Gill-over-ground, or ground ivy, is available year-round.

Location. Eastern United States, roughly to the Mississippi.

Cooking tips. Inedible except as strong-tasting, harshly aromatic medicinal tea made by drying leaves and steeping them in hot water for about 10 minutes.

Medicinal uses. Tea used to treat measles. The Chinese use it to clear fever, dissolve stones in urinary tract, stimulate circulation, reduce inflammation, treat influenza, and alleviate pain.

POKEWEED
(*Phytolacca americana*)

Description. Large leaves; reddish, coarse stems; greenish white flowers in clusters; purple black berries on stalk. Pokeweed, or poke, is found growing on waste ground almost anywhere in the United States.

Cooking tips. Very young leaves, as they first emerge, are edible after cooking in at least two changes of water.

Location. Entire United States, except extreme desert, southern California, and lower Florida.

WARNING. *Don't eat pokeweed unless foraging with a botanist. Root, stems, and berries of the plant are poisonous. See also appendix 2.*

Medicinal uses. Slightly narcotic, emetic, and purgative. Berries used as poultice on wounds and sores. Seeds and fruits steeped in water used to treat arthritis. Use only under medical supervision.

PEPPERWEED
(*Lepidium virginicum*)

Description. Flat seed pods, peppery taste; leaf lance shaped, toothed.

Location. Eastern United States, roughly to the Mississippi.

Cooking tips. Add seeds to salads. Young leaves are edible but bitter; use sparingly.

Medicinal uses. Tea from leaves and seeds is said to restore sex drive. Native Americans used the plant as a general medicinal.

WILD ASPARAGUS (*Asparagus officinalis*)

Description. Green spike when first emerges. Found along roadsides and fencerows. Locate asparagus in the fall, when large, feathery adult plants are easiest to see. Mark spot. Harvest the following spring.

Location. Entire United States, except extreme desert, southern California, and lower Florida.

WARNING. *Remember Wild Plant Foraging Rule #7: Road-side plants might be tainted with benzene, lead, oil, and other auto pollutants.*

Cooking tips. One favorite is asparagus roll-ups. Place three spears of asparagus on a flour tortilla. Cover asparagus with cheddar cheese, Miracle Whip, and bean sprouts. Roll up tortilla and microwave 35 seconds on high.

Medicinal uses. Asparagus is an excellent diuretic. Asparagine (that odor you smell when urinating) is antiseptic. Asparagusic acid is used to treat fluke infections, such as schistosomiasis.

R. crispus

DOCK (*Rumex orbiculatus, R. crispus, R. patientia*)

Description. The many varieties of dock are common weeds growing on disturbed ground, edges of fields, roadsides, and vacant lots. Leaves typically widest at base, narrow to tip, rounded at base; paperlike flower spikes; fruits three parted, brownish to red with three nutlets. Docks emerge in the spring, first as unfurling leaves, later the flower spike shoots up with smaller leaves attached. Flowers and eventually seeds cluster along the top several inches of the spikes. Swamp or water dock *(R. orbiculatus)* is found growing in water or along stream margins. It is stout and tall (to 6 feet) with a long root and flat, narrow, dark green leaves. Both curly dock *(R.crispus)* and yellow dock *(R. patientia)* have curly or wavy leaf margins.

Location. Entire United States, except extreme desert, southern California, and lower Florida.

WARNING. *Contains oxalic acid and, like spinach, should not be eaten more than twice a week.*

Cooking tips. Leaves and seeds edible. Tender young leaves, as they emerge, are most edible. Older leaves are tough and bitter and should be cooked in two changes of water. Steam, sauté, or stir-fry young leaves. Season with ginger, soy, lemon juice, and sesame seed oil. Leaves are great with walnuts and raisins. Dock seeds are edible in late summer and autumn. Hulled seeds can be ground into flour and used as a soup thickener or as a flour extender in baked goods.

Medicinal uses. Curly dock and yellow dock are used by naturopaths and mid-wives as a tea to treat anemia and raise iron levels in pregnant women. Iron in this form does not cause constipation. Curly dock and yellow dock root are also used with vinegar to treat ringworm. All dock roots are laxative, bitter digestive stimu-lants.

CINQUEFOIL (*Potentilla canadensis*)
SILVERWEED (*P. anserina*)

Description. Leaves on long, jointed stolons (delicate stemlike appendages). Two types of leaves: oval or elliptical (which are much smaller and have sharply toothed leaflets up to 1¼ inches long). Small buttercup-like flower. Both species can be found on waste ground or in gravely or sandy habitats.

P. canadensis

Location. *P. canadensis* is found in the eastern United States to the Mississippi. *P. anserina* is found on the West Coast.

Cooking tips. *P. canadensis* can be used to make a gold-colored tea that is high in calcium. For a quick roast, cook the leaves in a hot (covered) Dutch oven for 2 to 3 minutes. Pour boiling water over the leaves. *P. anserina* roots are edible. Gather the roots, wash them thoroughly, and steam in a wok. Native Americans steamed the roots in cedar boxes and served them with duck fat. To this day the Ditidaht peoples of British Columbia gather and prepare the roots in this traditional way.

Medicinal uses. Roots are rich in tannins and are used by some naturopathic physicians to treat diarrhea, Crohn's disease, colitis, gastritis, and peptic ulcers. Use only under the supervision of a trained holistic health care practitioner.

CARROT, QUEEN ANNE'S LACE (*Daucus carota*)

Description. Biennial. Fine, deeply dissected leaf. Second year's growth has white flower many call Queen Anne's lace. Root smells and tastes like domestic carrot but is tough and woody. High in vitamin A and fiber.

Location. Eastern United States, roughly to the Mississippi.

WARNING. *Hemlock look-alike (see appendix 2). Before using wild carrot, be certain that it has its characteristic carrot smell. Hemlock stems are purple spotted or purple blotched. When mature, hemlock is much taller than wild carrots. Remember Wild Plant Foraging Rule #1: When not certain of plant identification, follow the plant through a complete growth cycle or get expert advice before using.*

Cooking tips. Imparts a carrotlike flavor to vegetable stew. Eat soft tissue around root's pithy core. Florets can be stripped off head and sprinkled over salads. Also try them in meat loaf.

Medicinal uses. Root tea is antimicrobial, adiuretic, hypotensive, and a worm expellant. Animal studies show seed prevents ovum from implanting.

BURDOCK (*Arctium lappa, A. minus*)

Description. Large leaf, looks like elephant ear; large taproot. *A. minus* has a smaller leaf, flower, and flower spike. Common garden nuisance. In June or July dig first-year roots of this biennial.

Location. Throughout the United States, except extreme mountain and desert regions.

A. lappa

Cooking tips. Peel roots and cut into thin strips. Boil strips in water, sesame seed oil, ginger, and soy sauce. If bitter, use two changes of water. Serve hot under a pat of butter and dollop of low-fat sour cream.

Mock celery soup can be made with petioles of burdock. Add burdock, wild carrots, and wild onions to chicken stock. Cook, season, and serve. First-year young leaves can be scraped and eaten like celery.

Medicinal uses. Eighteenth-century treatment for gonorrhea and syphilis. Native Americans used for scurvy, sores, and rheumatism. Chinese use for tonsillitis and flu and as poultice on boils and abscesses. Seed extracts lower blood-sugar levels. Traditionally, boiled root used to reduce inflammation, control bacteria infection, and treat skin conditions.

BERGAMOT, BEE BALM (*Monarda fistulosa, M. didyma*)

Description. Leaves paired, oval to lance shaped; *M. fistulosa* has lavender flowers, florets resemble war bonnets, with strong oregano odor and flavor. *M. didyma's* red florets have a sweeter, pineapple flavor—a top-notch edible flower. Typically found on well-drained soil, along roadsides, and dry wood edges.

Location. Throughout the United States, except extreme mountain and desert regions.

Cooking tips. Eat young leaves raw, as they first emerge. *M. fistulosa* flowers have oregano-like taste; use flowers in salads or as tea; excellent over sauces, especially Italian. Also try the flowers in your favorite meat marinade—count on ½ cup flowers to 2 cups marinade. Infuse flowers and leaves in cold water with mint and lemon balm leaves. Refrigerate overnight. *M. didyma* florets are an excellent garnish to fruit dishes and teas.

M. fistulosa

Medicinal uses. Use the tea to treat colds, sore throats, fevers, and headaches. This expectorant prevents excess mucus and soothes bronchial complaints, sinusitis, digestive problems, and flatulence. Rub tea over skin eruptions. Ancient Native Americans drank the tea to relieve arthritis pain.

HAWTHORN (*Crataegus* spp.)

Description. Spiny shrubs to small, spiny trees; white flowers in terminal clusters, typically five petals; red berry fruit; leaves toothed, ovate, cut or lobed. Found in

wetlands, gardens, along wood edges, lawns.

Location. Various species found throughout the United States.

WARNING. *Uterine stimulate: May induce menstruation. Contraindicated for pregnant women.*

Cooking tips. Sweet-sour flavor. Eat the fruit and flowers in salads, stews, soups, and tea. Try eating them right off the tree in season (August and early September). Dried hawthorn berries can be purchased at Oriental drugstores or markets.

Medicinal uses. Bioflavonoid-rich hawthorn has been used to improve peripheral circulation to the heart, extremities, and brain. In Europe and China hawthorn has long been used to treat heart disease. It is also used by naturopathic physicians and others to treat angina, cardiac arrhythmia, heart disease, high blood pressure, and intermittent claudication (leg pain caused by partially occluded coronary arteries). In China the dried fruits are decocted and used for treating irritable bowel and gall bladder problems. Only with your physician's knowledge and approval: Eat the fruits raw for circulatory stimulation, or simmer the new leaves and flower buds to make hawthorn tea to treat heart conditions. In China dried hawthorn berries are given to infants suffering from indigestion from improper nursing technique.

JERUSALEM ARTICHOKE
(*Helianthus tuberosus*)

Description. Yellow sunflower; broad ovate, rough leaves, lower leaves opposite, upper leaves alternate; hairy stem; tuberous root. This plant can be found along roadsides. Add tubers to your garden and they'll provide a substantial food source that continues to reproduce year after year. Harvest tubers in fall and spring.

Location. Throughout the United States.

Cooking tips. Tuber can be peeled, sliced, and eaten raw. Has taste similar to water

chestnut. Also microwave, bake, or boil like a potato. This plant is worth looking for.

Medicinal uses. Tea made from flowers and leaves is a traditional treatment for arthritis. Inulin-rich tuber is slow to release sugars, making it a good food for diabetics.

CHICORY (*Cichorium intybus*)

Description. Leaves lanceshaped, deeply cut, dissected margins, stiff mid-vein spine; blue flower. Common along the shoulders of rural roads.

Location. Throughout the United States, except extreme mountain and desert regions.

Cooking tips. In New Orleans the dried root of chicory is ground and blended with coffee. Young leaves are edible, although bitter. Try combining them with ½ cup chicory blossoms and 1 pint low-fat cottage cheese.

Medicinal uses. Occasionally used as a nerve tonic, liver tonic, bitters, laxative. May reduce inflammation.

BLACK WILLOW (*Salix nigra*)
WEEPING WILLOW (*S. alba*)

Description. Tree or shrub; lancelike, fine-toothed leaves. Prefers wet ground.

Location. Throughout the United States.

WARNING. *Willow contains salicin. Too much salicin may be dangerous. Consult your physician before trying this tea.*

Medicinal uses. Willow tea can be made from stems and leaves. Drop willow cuttings into hot water. Steep for 1 minute for a relaxing brew that may take the edge off an aching head. The salicin found in willow and

S. alba

in many other plants is the natural chemical model for synthetic aspirin. Aspirin may help prevent acute infections, cancer, and heart attacks.

STINGING NETTLE
(*Urtica dioica*)

Description. Hairy stem and leaves; hairs sting; leaves lancelike, sharply toothed. Common resident along roadsides, fields, and wooded areas. Fine, stinging hairs contain skin irritant that is destroyed when plant is cooked. Nettles are high in vitamins A and C, are fiber rich, and a great mineral source.

Location. Throughout the United States.

WARNING. *Don't confuse the hairy cells of stinging nettle with the thorny, poisonous horse nettle (see appendix 2).*

Cooking tips. Stinging nettle is one of my favorite foods. In the spring I sauté the young shoots with dandelions. In the summer and fall the new growth—the whorl of new leaves on the end of stems—can be picked, chopped, and stir-fried. Chopped leaves can be rolled up in a wonton with chopped celery, carrot, ginger root, and flax seeds. Steam wontons for 5 minutes, then dip in 4 tablespoons low-sodium soy sauce and 2 tablespoons sesame seed oil. Cook with wild carrot, wild leeks, dandelion greens, watercress, and soy sauce. Boil older plants, then throw away the plants and use nettle stock for soups or as a refreshing vitamin-rich drink. Plant can be harvested throughout the year. Simply cut off top new leaf generation for eating.

Medicinal uses. Tea may combat diarrhea. Diuretic in decoction. Herbalists rubbed whole plant over arthritic joints and muscles as counterirritant. Freeze-dried nettles may relieve hay fever.

WOOLLY MULLEIN
(*Verbascum thapsus*)

Description. Large, hairy, Velcro-like leaf; yellow flower; biennial; prostrate first year, erect second year. Grows in vacant lots. Native Americans lined moccasins with the warm, woolly leaf.

Location. Throughout the United States.

Medicinal uses. Tea from leaves and flowers used as a folk or naturopathic remedy to treat coughs, colds, bronchitis, and other upper-respiratory problems. Hairy leaves used to rub out pain of stinging nettle. Mountain folk healers use mullein flowers, Epsom salts, and vinegar to wash necrotic wounds of recluse spider bite.

YELLOW SORREL, GARDEN SORREL (*Oxalis stricta*)

Description. Shamrocklike leaf, deeply dissected into three round lobes; yellow flower. Wood sorrel and garden sorrel leaves, flowers, and seeds have a sour taste. Common in many gardens

Location. Eastern United States, roughly to the Mississippi.

WARNING. *High in oxalic acid. Use this plant sparingly. Excessive consumption may inhibit the body's absorption of calcium.*

Cooking tips. Add yellow flowers, seeds, and leaves to salads—or brew them into a beverage.

Medicinal uses. The Chinese use the *Oxalis* species to clear fevers, resolve clots, and reduce swelling. Also used as snakebite treatment.

SHEEP SORREL (*Rumex acetosella*)

Description. Thick, succulent, sour-tasting leaves; long, pointed, tapered tip, with short, pointed basal lobes. Found on waste ground, wood margins, gardens. Available spring and fall.

Location. Throughout the United States.

WARNING. *High in oxalic acid (see yellow sorrel).*

Cooking tips. Prepare like wood sorrel. Eat sparingly.

Medicinal uses. This is one of the ingredients in the traditional Essiac anticancer formula that combines burdock root, sheep sorrel, red clover, rhubarb root, kelp, slippery elm bark, watercress, and blessed thistle.

WILD GARLIC
(*Allium sativum*)

Description. Long, narrow, pencil-like leaf stalk; flower head bears small green plantlets that drop off and propagate.

Location. Throughout the United States.

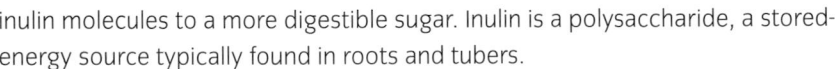

Cooking tips. Always cook wild garlic and wild onions to cleave inulin molecules to a more digestible sugar. Inulin is a polysaccharide, a stored-energy source typically found in roots and tubers.

Medicinal uses. Wild garlic, chives, and onions may reduce blood pressure, lower cholesterol, lower blood sugar, and protect you from acute infections such as a cold or the flu.

DAYLILY (*Hemerocallis fulva*)

Description. Yellow, tuberous roots; long, narrow, lancelike leaves; orange lily flower. Found along roadsides. Transplant to clean soil away from auto pollution. Common in many gardens.

Location. Throughout the United States.

WARNING. *Use plant only when in bloom. Early growth resembles poisonous iris shoots (see appendix 2); daylily's yellowish tubers are distinctive.*

Cooking tips. The strong-tasting flowers are flavonoid rich. Daylily petals can be teased apart from the whole flower and tossed in with salad greens. Flowers and unopened buds can be stir-fried or batter-dipped and cooked tempura style. Try the sautéed flowers wrapped in wontons, steamed. The Japanese Sauce (see page 21) makes a great wonton dip. Buds can be steamed, boiled, or deep-fried. Serve with butter or cheese sauce. Firm root tubers can be harvested all year. Add raw to salads or cook like a potato.

MILKWEED
(*Asclepias syriaca*)

Description. Sticky white sap; large egglike seed pods; large ovate leaves. Common milkweed is sometimes eaten as a cooked vegetable—but the sap contains toxins.

Location. Eastern United States, roughly to the Mississippi.

WARNING. *I have included milkweed as an edible plant because many people eat it. Like pokeweed, milkweed is potentially dangerous without special processing and cooking preparation. All parts of the plant may contain heart-stimulating cardiac glycosides. I recommend you not eat milkweed unless it is prepared by a knowledgeable and experienced forager. There are several species, some more edible than others. There is poor documentation on appropriate preparation. I would only eat this plant in a survival situation where no other food was available. See also appendix 2.*

Cooking tips. All edible parts of this plant are best cooked. I eat the young shoots, unopened flower buds, and thrice-cooked seed pods. It is safest to steep plant parts in at least two changes (preferably three changes) of water to reduce cardiac glycoside, a potential toxin.

Medicinal uses. Sap used to treat warts, moles, and ringworm. Boiled roots used to treat sterility, asthma, and dysentery.

GROUND-CHERRY, LANTERN PLANT
(*Physalis pubescens, P. ixocarpa*)

Description. Hairy stems and leaves; pale green plant. Sometimes called lantern plant because of the lanternlike husk. Ground-cherries can be harvested when ripe, usually in August or September.

Location. Entire United States, except extreme desert, southern California, and lower Florida.

P. ixocarpa

WARNING. *Unripe berries may make a few sick. Avoid this fruit and other member of the nightshade family. The horse nettle is a toxic look-alike (see appendix 2).*

Cooking tips. The Amish in my neighborhood pick wild ground-cherries and bake them into wonderful pies. You can purchase this plant from Richter's (see appendix 3). Plant the seeds in your garden, then harvest ground-cherries in fall. By purchasing the plants from a reliable source and then planting them, you can be assured you are eating ground-cherries and not a toxic look-alike, such as horse nettle. *P. ixocarpa* are available in many Mexican markets.

Medicinal uses. Used by the Chinese as poultice over abscesses and as a vermicide and cough sedative.

YELLOW GOAT'S-BEARD, MEADOW SALSIFY (*Tragopogon pratensis*)

Description. Yellow Goat's-beard looks like a large dandelion: yellow flowers; large, deeply and sharply serrated leaves.

Location. Entire United States, except extreme desert, southern California, and lower Florida.

Cooking tips. Root edible when boiled and then fried.

Medicinal uses. Apply cooled infusion of plant to boils. Use as a gargle for sore throat treatment.

PRICKLY LETTUCE (*Lactuca serriola*)

Description. Lettucelike; white, sticky juice in stems and leaves; leaves alternate, lancelike, toothed and spiny margin; small yellow flowers in clusters.

Location. Throughout the United States.

Cooking tips. Blanched leaves are bitter. Definitely won't impress dinner guests.

Medicinal uses. Was used as cough suppressant. About 200 years ago distilled *L. serriola* and wild opium *(Lactuca canadensis)* were used as a very weak, opiumlike sedative.

RED CLOVER (*Trifolium pratense*)

Description. Often three leaflets showing pale chevron; round flower head; rose purple flower petals.

Location. Throughout the United States.

Cooking tips. Petals can be batter-fried or eaten raw in salads.

Medicinal uses. Tea from flowers is flavonoid rich, providing antioxidant, anti-cancer protection. Skilled herbalists used this plant to treat cuts, burns, and liver ailments. Integral part of the Essiac anti-cancer formula consisting of burdock root, slippery elm bark, rhubarb root, watercress, sheep sorrel, blessed thistle, red clover, and kelp.

SPIDERWORT (*Tradescantia virginiana*)

Description. Flower violet, three round petals, long golden stamens; long, lanced leaves. Common along roadsides.

Location. Entire United States, except extreme desert, southern California, and lower Florida.

Cooking tips. The strong-tasting young shoots and leaves can be eaten but are mucilaginous. The little flowers bloom every morning all summer long. I like them

uncooked in an omelet or sprinkled in a floral salad.

Medicinal uses. Pouliced root rubbed on skin cancer. Tea for stomachache. Long leaves used to bind wounds. Antiseptic. The flowers may relieve congestion due to summer heat and humidity. The slimy texture should release and thin mucus, a reflex action due to the polysaccharides in the flower.

COMFREY (*Symphytum officinale*)

Description. Leaves large, elongated, hairy, prickly; stalks hollow, hairy; flower fingerlike, pale white. Found on moist, low ground.

Location. This plant has escaped gardens and is found nationwide.

WARNING. *This plant may be carcinogenic. May contain pyrrolizidine alkaloids that damage the liver. Avoid eating this plant, especially the roots. Dried leaves have lowest amount of the alkaloids. Although the alkaloids are concentrated in the root, they are found throughout the plant. I have included this plant as it was once a favorite of foragers and folk medicine practitioners. I do not recommend eating it.*

Medicinal uses. Plant parts demulcent, astringent. Native Americans used tea for dysentery, gonorrhea, and heartburn. Holistic practitioners use the herb internally to treat stomach ulcers and irritable bowel syndrome and externally to mend sprains and broken bones.

PEPPERMINT (*Mentha piperita*)

Description. Peppermint, like spearmint, is found along wet lowlands, streams, and lakes. It has a square stem, like most members of the mint family, with opposite leaves, sharply serrated. Crushed plant has strong aromatic odor of mint.

Location. Eastern United States, roughly to the Mississippi.

Cooking tips. Use the flowers in salads and the leaves to flavor cold drinks such as cold infusion tea (sun tea). Used in many Middle Eastern foods. Try it in rice and tabbouleh.

Medicinal uses. Oil used to treat colic. Tea used to treat colds, fever, and headache. Excellent digestive aid. Whole plant crushed and rubbed on skin to reduce pain and sensitivity.

CHAMOMILE (*Matricaria recutita, Chamaemelum nobilis*)

Description. Hairy stem; narrow leaflets divided into many segments; flower on long, erect stem, yellow white florets. Aromatic. German chamomile *(M. recutita)* is the herb of choice, as it's more pleasant tasting than Roman chamomile *(C. nobilis).* Found in sandy soil in full sun.

M. recutita

Location. Eastern United States, roughly to the Mississippi.

WARNING. *Overdosage may cause vomiting. Similar to ragweed pollen— may trigger allergies.*

Medicinal uses. Flower makes excellent tea—a soothing, relaxing brew sometimes taken for indigestion. Available over the counter. Tea used for treating children's colic (see physician first). Bioflavonoid rich; useful against hay fever and asthma. Use externally for eczema.

YARROW, MILFOIL (*Achillea millefolium*)

Description. Creeping or erect herb. Leaves featherlike, slightly hairy, divided into

fine leaflets; white or pinkish flower. Aromatic. Found in open sun or partial shade.

Location. Eastern United States, roughly to the Mississippi.

WARNING. *Yarrow looks similar to poison hemlock (see appendix 2). Get expert identification.*

Medicinal uses. Was used as poultice over wounds. Tea used to treat colds. Dried yarrow leaves cooked in lard makes an excellent wound dressing.

ASIATIC DAYFLOWER (*Commelina communis*)

Description. Common weed in many gardens. Erect stems collapse on themselves as they grow (up to 3 feet). Deep blue flowers, ½ to ¾ inch wide, two rounded petals (like Mickey Mouse ears) with a small white petal behind the pair. Flower's ovary sheathed in three green sepals; six yellow-tipped stamens. Fleshy, oblong leaves, 3 to 5 inches long, pointed tips. Leaves sheath stem.

Location. Found nationwide. Alien weed: originally from China.

Cooking tips. This free food comes up late every year. Young leaves and shoots can be added to salads. We get so many of these plants in our garden that I pull whole shoots, wash them, and add them to stir-fries. Entire flower is edible. As fruit matures, the seed capsule (tucked in the sepal sheath) is a crunchy treat. In late summer flowers keep coming. You can eat seed pods for a healthful dose of essential oils and phytosterols.

Medicinal uses. In China the leaf tea is used as a sore throat gargle, for urinary infections, acute intestinal enteritis, and dysentery. Tea is also used to reduce fevers, as a detoxicant, and as a diuretic (to treat edema from join swelling and pain from arthritis). Flowers contain isoflavones and phytosterols. Seeds contain fatty acids and essential and nonessential amino acids.

AMARANTH
(*Amaranthus* spp.)

Description. Amaranth, sometimes referred to as red root, is a hairy, stout weed; leaves ovate to lance shaped on long stalks; flowers in dense clusters, bristly. Seeds typically black. Flowers in July and August, seeds available soon after.

Location. Roadsides, fields, waste ground east and west of the Mississippi at lower elevations.

Cooking tips. Young shoots and leaves eaten raw or cooked. May be dried and reconstituted in hot water for winter food. Seeds used whole as cooked cereal. Seeds ground into flour and used to supplement flour for bread, muffins, etc. Seed also added whole to bread, pancakes, and waffles. Pinole (atole) is a hot corn drink made with toasted amaranth seeds and roasted blue or white cornmeal. Spread cornmeal and amaranth seeds on a cookie sheet or aluminum foil. Toast in 425°F oven for 8 to 10 minutes. Add sugar and cinnamon and stir into hot milk, simmer for 15 minutes. Native Americans ate leaves and seeds mixed with grease and cooked. Try a mixed-greens dish of young and tender amaranth leaves combined with mustard, plantain, dock, and nettle, and cooked with bacon.

Medicinal uses. Native Americans used this plant mixed with green corn in sacred rituals. Leaves are astringent and used to stem profuse menstruation. Decoction of the plant used with doll likeness of an enemy to inflict cancer.

CHAPTER FOUR

Woodlands

HEPATICA, AMERICAN LIVERWORT
(*Hepatica americana*)

Description. Perennial plant; leaves on long hairy petiole, shaped like three lobes of liver; white, blue, or purplish flower appears early. One of the first flowers to bloom in March or April.

Location. Entire United States, except extreme desert, southern California, and lower Florida.

WARNING. *Large amounts of hepatica are poisonous. Use is reserved for a skilled herbalist. See also appendix 2.*

Medicinal uses. Small amounts of roots and leaves used to treat indigestion and disorders of the kidneys, gall bladder, and liver. I have used a water extraction of the root to repel mosquitoes.

SKUNK CABBAGE (*Symplocarpus foetidus*, *Lysichitum americanum*)

Description. Plant smells like a skunk when damaged; leaves large, smooth margins; primitive spathe (flower) emerges before leaves. The plant is found in wet lowlands and woods. Not edible. The spathe of western skunk cabbage (*L. americanum*) is bright yellow.

Location. S. foetidus is found in the eastern United States, while western skunk cabbage is found west of the Rockies.

WARNING. *Skunk cabbage is poisonous and contains oxalate. Juice from the fresh plant may cause skin blistering and will severely burn digestive tract if eaten. Only experts should handle this plant. I have included this plant because it is a common woodland plant, is striking in appearance, and has a startling odor. Although its name suggests that it is edible, it requires exhaustive preparation In several changes of cooking water to yield mediocre results. Botanically, it is unique: It actually produces heat that often melts snow around its base. In Michigan it is the earliest flowering plant of spring. See also appendix 2.*

S. foetidus

Medicinal uses. Native Americans used *Symplocarpus* roots as a medicinal. First the roots were thoroughly dried to crystallize burning oxalate. Infusion or tea from the dried root was used as a mild sedative. The sap of *Lysichitum,* western skunk cabbage, was used to treat ringworm.

MARSH MARIGOLD, COWSLIP (Caltha palustris)

Description. Leaves ovate; distinctive fluorescent yellow flowers. Thrives in sunlight to partial shade. Plants grow in low wetlands.

Location. Entire United States, except extreme desert, southern California, and lower Florida.

WARNING. *In view of the caustic nature of this plant, best to avoid it. Use it as a survival food only.*

Cooking tips. Leaves eaten as a potherb in the spring before the flowers open. This is a risky practice, as it must be cooked in several changes of water. Leaves are extremely bitter and not worth the time and trouble.

Medicinal uses. Leaves used as laxative and cough syrup. Root used in decoction for colds.

JACK-IN-THE-PULPIT, INDIAN TURNIP (*Arisaema triphyllum*)

Description. Leaves compound, three leaflets, oval, smooth, lighter underside; distinctive primitive flower, spadix in pulpitlike spathe. Indian turnip is found in rich soils, generally a woods or shady lowland.

Location. Entire United States, except extreme desert, southern California, and lower Florida.

WARNING. *Do not eat fresh plant. Like skunk cabbage, it contains caustic oxalates when fresh and must be thoroughly dried before use. Not recommended. Handle with care: Calcium oxalate will cause painful burns in cracked skin or open sores. See also appendix 2.*

Cooking tips. Native Americans sliced roots and dried them, deactivating calcium oxalate. Dried root was cooked and eaten like potato chips.

Medicinal uses. Plant parts used in treatment of cough, sore throat, and ringworm. Also as a poultice for boils and abscesses.

MAYAPPLE (*Podophyllum peltatum*)

Description. Large pair of dissected, parasol-like leaves; white flower on petiole between leaves; yellow green fruit. Mayapple is, for the most part, poisonous. The two large, parasol-like leaves shelter a white flower that bears an edible fruit when ripe in midsummer. Pick the fruit when soft and ripe.

Location. Entire United States, except extreme desert, southern California, and lower Florida.

WARNING. *Except for the pulp of the ripe fruit, this plant is poisonous. See also appendix 2.*

Cooking tips. Expert foragers carefully gather ripe fruit for use in pie fillings and jellies.

Medicinal uses. Etoposide, the active agent of mayapple, may be useful treating testicular and small lung cancer.

WHITE TRILLIUM
(*Trillium grandiflorum*)

Description. Leaves, sepals, and flower petals in threes. There are several varieties of trillium. Leaves and red to purple flowers are edible but, for my taste, members of this genus are too pretty to eat. Trillium and toadshade (a red-flowered species) are easy to grow in the home garden. Locate in shade and rich soil.

Location. Entire United States, except extreme desert, southern California, and lower Florida.

Medicinal uses. Native Americans used *T. grandiflorum* root bark decoction for earsores, and splinters of wood soaked in root extraction were pricked through the skin over arthritic joints.

RAMPS, WILD LEEKS
(*Allium tricoccum*)

Description. Strong onion aroma; long, wide leaves grow directly from bulb. Found on banks and in wet woods.

Location. Eastern United States, roughly to the Mississippi.

Cooking tips. Leaves, stems, and bulbs are edible. Marvelous in stews and soup,

or sautéed with soy sauce, extra virgin olive oil, and a little water to keep plants from sticking to pan.

Medicinal uses. Used as a tonic to combat colds. Disputed evidence that eating raw bulbs may reduce risk of heart disease. Chop leaves into chicken soup to potentiate this cold and flu fighter.

FIDDLEHEAD FERNS
(*Matteuccia* and *Pteretis* spp.)

Description. Fiddleheads are the unfurled, early-growth leaves of ferns (tightly wound like a fiddlehead).

Location. Eastern United States, roughly to the Mississippi River.

WARNING. *Some ferns, such as bracken fern, may cause stomach cancer. Eating too many fiddleheads may lead to thiamine deficiency. Taste them, don't feast on them.*

Pteretis spp.

Cooking tips. Can be eaten raw or steamed. I prefer them sautéed or deep-fried. You can buy fiddleheads at Native American restaurants in Seattle and Vancouver. This is where you should begin your experience with eating ferns.

WILD GINGER
(*Asarum canadense*)

Description. Aromatic root, smells like ginger; two heart-shaped leaves; note the hairy stem and leaves; primitive flower emerges in May. Found on rich soil in moist woods.

Location. Entire United States, except extreme desert, southern California, and lower Florida.

Cooking tips. Crushed root can be added to salad dressings. When dried and grated it is an adequate substitute for oriental ginger. For the daring gourmet, try boiling the root until tender and then simmer in maple syrup. The result is an unusual candy treat.

Medicinal uses. Root traditionally used to treat colds and cough; antiseptic and tonic.

SWEET CICELY, WILD ANISE (*Myrrhis odorata*)

Description. Broken root smells like anise. Bright green, shiny leaves; small white flowers in umbels. Wild anise, commonly called sweet cicely, has a sweet anise odor and taste. Use as an anise substitute.

Location. Entire United States, except extreme desert, southern California, and lower Florida.

WARNING. *Looks like poison hemlock (see appendix 2).*

Cooking tips. Use root to spice cooked greens. Leaves can be added to salads.

Medicinal use. Leaves occasionally eaten by diabetics as sugar substitute

PARTRIDGEBERRY, SQUAW VINE (*Mitchella repens*)

Description. A tiny creeper with oval leaves, found at the base of trees in wet woods of the northern and central United States and Canada. Bland berry ripens to bright red by late summer.

Location. Eastern, northern, and central United States.

Cooking tips. A tasteless trail food with little or no bulk—a hard-times survival berry, available all winter.

Medicinal uses. Pioneers used the dried leaf tea to treat menstrual pain and regulate menses. Aerial parts of plant were used as a cleansing, soothing wash for sore nipples and arthritis.

WINTERGREEN
(*Gaultheria procumbens*)

Description. Evergreen; long oval leaves, finely serrated margins; drooping white flowers. The flower forms an edible berry that turns from white to red by late summer. Available all winter—if not gobbled up by late-season foragers.

Location. Entire United States, except extreme desert, southern California, and lower Florida. There are several species of this plant in North America. Creeping wintergreen, or checkerberry, is found in the eastern half of the United States.

WARNING. *Over-the-counter concentrations of the essential oil of wintergreen may be toxic.*

Cooking tips. Add summer fruits to pancake and muffin mixes. Use the leaves to make a delicate tea or munch them (don't swallow) as a breath freshener.

Medicinal uses. Astringent and counterirritant. Never take oil internally. Tea from leaves has been used for flu and colds, and as a stomach alkalizer.

SPICEBUSH
(*Lindera benzoin*)

Description. Shrub found in rich woodlands and along streams. Grows to 15 feet, with numerous spreading branches. Smooth branches give off spicy odor when soft bark is scratched with thumbnail. Leaves smooth, bright green, pointed (widest near or above middle section), simple, alternate, deciduous, 2½ to 5½ inches long and 1½ to 2½ inches wide. Flowers small,

yellow, in dense clusters along previous year's twigs. Fruits in clusters, widest in middle (somewhat football shaped, but with more rounded ends), start out green and become bright red in autumn. Flowers appear in early spring, before leaves.

Location. Eastern United States, roughly to the Mississippi.

Cooking tips. In the spring I gather end twigs, tie them together with string, and throw them in a pot with leeks, nettles, mushrooms, and dandelions. Bundles of stems can be steeped in boiling water to make tea (sweeten with honey). Young leaves can be used in the same way. In the fall, try drying the fruits in a food dryer. Dry fruits are hard and can be ground in a coffee mill and used as a substitute for allspice.

Medicinal uses. Native Americans used the bark in infusion for treating colds, coughs, and dysentery. Tea made from the bark was used as a spring tonic. Bathing in this tea reportedly helps rheumatism. Tea made from the twigs was used to treat dysmenorrhea.

CLEAVERS, BEDSTRAW
(*Galium aparine*)

Description. Weak, slender stem; eight leaves in whorl; tiny white flowers. Found in woodlands, along streams, and in vacant lots.

Location. Eastern United States, roughly to the Mississippi.

Cooking tips. Also called bedstraw, cleaver leaves can be added to salads in early spring. Mature leaves are tough and must be cooked. Seeds of summer can be roasted and ground into coffee substitute. It's better than chicory but far short of coffee.

Medicinal uses. Diuretic. Tea used for skin diseases such as psoriasis, seborrhea, and eczema. Whole plant's juice is taken internally for kidney stones and cancer.

YELLOW MOREL MUSHROOM (*Morchella esculenta*)
BLACK MOREL (*Morchella elata*)

M. esculenta

Description. Convoluted gray or black brainlike flesh. Found from mid-April through May in many wooded areas. Convoluted brain look is distinctive, but there are some dangerous look-alikes.

Location. Eastern United States, roughly to the Mississippi.

WARNING. *Many mushrooms are deadly. Seek positive identification from an expert before eating.*

PUFFBALL MUSHROOM
(*Calvatia gigantea*)

Description. Golfball-to-basketball-size mushroom; fleshy white throughout. Puffball is found on rich soil in shady areas.

Location. Eastern United States, roughly to the Mississippi.

WARNING. *Before eating, cut open and be certain flesh is white and not yellow. Also avoid this plant if gills or a rudimentary stem are inside.*

Immature puffball

Cooking tips. Can be cooked and eaten like an edible mushroom. Prepare sliced puffball in satay sauce, then stir-fry with vegetables and tofu. Slices can also be sautéed in butter.

AVALANCHE LILY, YELLOW AVALANCHE LILY
(*Erythronium grandiflorum*)

Description. Leaves lance and ellipse shaped, narrowing at base; deeply buried, edible corm; single yellow flower (sometimes two) on 7- or 8-inch stem (July). Found in alpine meadows and high slopes in western mountains. Similar to, and from the same genus as, the trout lily and the white dogtooth violet of the eastern United States.

Location. Mountainous West, primarily the Sierras and Rockies.

WARNING. *The corm contains the polysaccharide inulin and thus must be cooked to be edible.*

Cooking tips. Reaching the corm is a difficult dig, and much effort is needed. Native Americans wrapped the bulbs in cattails and reeds, then cooked them in an earth-filled pit over which a fire was burned. Ten to twelve hours in the pit would render the corms both edible and delicious.

Medicinal use. I believe the inulin-rich bulb would be helpful to diabetics. (In Japan the inulin in burdock root is used to treat diabetics.)

SPRING BEAUTY (*Claytonia caroliniana*)
INDIAN POTATO (*C. lanceolata*)
MOUNTAIN POTATO (*C. tuberosa*)

C. caroliniana

Description. Approximately 7 inches tall; narrow, lance-shaped leaves die off after bloom; flowers 1 centimeter across, light pink to white or white with pink veins, in loose terminal clusters, numbering from three to eighteen. Plant grows from ground where it is attached to an acorn-size, fleshy corm. Emerges and blooms in early spring. Found in rich, moist woods throughout the East and across the northern tier of United States and the mountainous West.

Location. Entire United States, except extreme desert, southern California, lower Florida, and the prairie states.

Cooking tips. The brown-skinned corm is edible. Peel the skin, wash, and eat raw or cooked. Try it on the grill with roasted vegetables. Roll the corm in olive oil, then roast for about 8 minutes until browned. Flowers are edible but bland.

TROUT LILY
(*Erythronium americanum*)

Description. Trout lily or white dog-tooth violet (*E. albidum*) has mottled leaves and small, yellow, lilylike flower. Avalanche lilies (of the mountainous West) are close relatives with edible bulbs.

Location. Eastern United States, roughly to the Mississippi.

Cooking tips. Young leaves may be boiled for 10 minutes and eaten, but they are poor tasting. The tuberous root is also edible after lengthy boiling. The real beauty of this plant is in the eyes of the beholder—as a foodstuff it's best left alone.

Medicinal uses. Tea from root used to reduce fever. Crushed leaves used as poultice over ulcers.

AMERICAN GINSENG (*Panax quinquefolius*)

Description. Straight, erect stem, with two or three leaf stems; five to eleven leaves per stem. American ginseng root, a prized medicinal in China, sells for about $300 per pound. Commercially cultivated.

Location. Eastern United States, roughly to the Mississippi.

Cooking tips. The Chinese cook the root in chicken soup. They also eat the berries. Dried root can be ground in an old-fashioned sausage grinder.

Medicinal uses. Ginseng root's active ingredients are called saponins (glycosides). Some saponins raise blood pressure, others lower it; some raise blood sugar, some lower it. Obviously, more research is needed. Today saponins from ginseng are being tested in preliminary studies as an anticancer chemotherapy.

EVENING PRIMROSE
(*Oenothera biennis*)

Description. Biennial, second-year erect plant; yellow flower; leaves lanceshaped, pointed tip, fine-toothed margin. Evening primrose is found in fields bordering wooded areas.

Location. Eastern United States, roughly to the Mississippi.

Cooking tips. The flowers, roots, and seeds are edible. Dip flowers in egg whites, roll them in sugar, then deep-fry. Also try cooking them in a stir-fry or spreading them in salads.

Medicinal uses. Plant parts contain gamma-linolenic acid (GLA). GLA may prevent acne, alcoholism, obesity, and schizophrenia (as yet unproven). My wife has had success relieving PMS with the oil of this plant's seeds.

CANDIED EVENING PRIMROSE

2 tablespoons high-proof alcohol (such as Everclear)
1 egg white
sugar

Whip together alcohol and egg white. Dip flowers. Sprinkle a thin layer of sugar on a cookie sheet. Fill a salt shaker with sugar, then sprinkle the sugar over the egg white–laden flowers. If you're handy with chopsticks, you can rotate the flower as you coat it with sugar. Lay the flowers on the cookie sheet and let them dry. Try candied flowers in tea or cordials, or use to garnish a dessert plate. All edible flowers can be candied. Also try this recipe with rose petals and violets. Yields two dozen flowers.

GROUNDNUT
(*Apios americana*)

Description. Climbing, pealike plant vine; numerous tubers along length of root; leaves alternate, compound, featherlike; seeds in long pods. Groundnut grows on wet ground, along the fringes of streams, bogs, and thickets. Easily transferable to your garden, where they can be harvested in the autumn or spring.

Location. Entire United States, except extreme desert, southern California, and lower Florida.

Cooking tips. Seeds are edible. Cook them like lentils. Tubers of *Apios* are 15 percent protein—a great potato substitute. Native Americans established settlements near this staple—a high-protein foraging food.

SASSAFRAS
(*Sassafras albidum*)

Description. Small tree with aromatic limbs, leaves, and roots. The leaves usually have two or three lobes and are alternate. There are many sucker plants growing adventitiously from the parent plant.

Location. Eastern and southern United States.

WARNING. *Sassafras oils may be carcinogenic (contains traces of the carcinogen safrole). Use judiciously.*

Cooking tips. Boil root, sweeten, and drink. Dried leaves as a spice.

Medicinal uses. Sassafras tea used as a diuretic and stimulant. Leaves and bark made into a tea and rubbed on the body may work as a mosquito repellent. Decoction from root was used as a tea substitute during colonial times.

PAWPAW (*Asimina triloba*)

Description. Small tree (10 to 25 feet) growing on riverbanks, along streams; often a secondary growth under taller trees. Leaves are alternate, simple, large (up to 12 inches), narrow at base and broad near tip.

Location. Eastern and southern United States.

Cooking tips. Large fruit can be eaten raw. Or remove seeds, cook like pudding, and blend with yogurt.

Medicinal use. An anticancer substance has been isolated from pawpaw that is more than 1,000 times as potent as the synthetic drug adriamycin.

APPLE, CRAB APPLE (*Malus* and *Pyrus* spp.)

Description. Small trees to 30 feet; flowers white, rosy white; fruit smaller than domestic apples. Some species have thorns.

Location. Throughout the United States.

Cooking tips. Sour, acid taste. Cook with sugar or honey. Make preserve with raspberries, blueberries, or blackberries.

Medicinal uses. Fruit can be cooked and eaten for colds.

Malus spp.

OAKS AND ACORNS (*Quercus* spp.)

Description. This is a large genera with species worldwide. *Note:* The best way to get acquainted with and learn how to identify oaks is to visit an arboretum, where the oaks are labeled for easy identification.

Location. Throughout the United States and southern Canada.

Q. alba

In the United States, I prefer acorns from the oaks that have rounded instead of pointed leaf lobes. White oak, bur oak, swamp chestnut oak, and chestnut oak are good examples from the eastern United States. The chinquapin oak, or yellow chestnut oak, also has sweet acorns. Out west look for live oak, blue oak, and Oregon white oak. Oaks with pointed leaves have more tannins and are too bitter to consume, even after special preparation.

Cooking tips. All oak nuts can be

improved by an overnight soaking in fresh water (to leach out bitter-tasting tannins). Native Americans would shell, crack, or smash the acorns, then place them in a skin bag and soak them in a stream for a day or two to remove the tannins. A quick solution in the kitchen is to puree the acorn meat in water. Using a blender, combine 1 cup water with every cup of nut meat. Blend thoroughly. Then press the water out of the nut meat through cheesecloth (or a clean pair of nylons or a white sock). I like the acorn puree on baked

Q. rubra

potatoes, over tomato sauce, in all baking recipes, or out of hand as a snack.

Medicinal uses. White oak has tannin-rich bark. While bitter tasting, tannins are also antiseptic and astringent. Native Americans and pioneers made tea from the bark and used it to treat mouth sores, burns, cuts, and scrapes. Many considered the bark a panacea. The Iroquois scraped powered bark from healed-over broken oak branches and sprinkled it over the navel of infants to heal the area after removal of the umbilical cord. They also used red oak bark decoction for diarrhea. Once again, the tannins account for the reported effectiveness of this remedy.

SUGAR MAPLE (*Acer saccharum*)
RED MAPLE (*A. rubrum*)

Description. Tree leaves resemble basic form of Canada's national emblem, typically three lobes (red maple leaves have distinctive red petioles); tree crowns are broad and rounded in the open; bark is smooth when young and furrows with age; seeds have characteristic helicopter-blade appearance and fly accordingly.

A. saccharum

Location. Various species found throughout the United States and southern Canada.

Cooking tips. Seeds may be eaten but are poor tasting. Pluck the seeds from the helicopter-blade husk and cook or stir-fry like peas.

Medicinal uses. Maple syrup is a glucose-rich sugar substitute with the added benefit of numerous minerals. Use it as a sweetener in place of sugar (which has no minerals). Traditionally maple syrup has been used to flavor and sweeten cough syrups. The unfinished fresh sap is considered a mineral-rich tonic. I store a couple gallons in the freezer and keep one in the refrigerator as a water source that—for flavor and nutrition—beats bottled spring water.

A. rubrum

BIGLEAF MAPLE (*Acer macrophyllum*)

Description. Large-leafed maple of the Pacific Northwest. Tree is understory dweller with five-lobed maplelike leaves. Leaves opposite, dark green above, pale green underneath; greenish yellow flowers hang in clusters. Fruit golden brown winged seeds in pairs.

Location. Dry and moist sites of Pacific Northwest forests. Often found with Douglas fir and cedar.

Cooking tips. Tree tapped for sap and made into syrup and sugar. Seeds may be boiled and eaten. Leaves used to flavor wild game, typically as a covering for meat cooked in a pit. Native Americans sprouted and ate young seed shoots (the sprouted cotyledons are bitter).

Medicinal uses. Leaf bud oil massaged in hair as a dressing. Raw sap was once considered a tonic.

MAPLE SAP TAP

Maple sugar and maple syrup from the winter and spring sap is what these trees are all about. For taps or information on where they can be purchased, contact a maple sugar mill near you.

Using a brace and a ⅜-inch bit, drill through the bark until you hit hardwood. Clean the hole thoroughly, then use a hammer to drive in the tap. For trees under 10 inches wide, use only one tap. For larger trees you may use two or three taps in a circle around the tree. Use a covered pail to collect the sap. If you're going to boil down the sap on an open fire, make sure that your wood is dry, as smoke will give the syrup an undesirable flavor. I use three pans over a long, narrow fire pit, pouring the sugar water from pan to pan as it cooks. Pan number one receives the fresh water from the trees, pan two receives the reduced water from pan one, and pan three receives the further reduced water from pan two. Pan three, of course, will have the thickest, richest water. Boil the syrup in pan three until it is thick enough to coat a spoon.

Sap flows best on warm sunny days after a freezing night. In southern Michigan tapping begins in late January and continues until mid-April, when the sap runs dark, thick, and stingy.

A few other trees that can be tapped for sap include black walnut and white, black, and yellow birch. Grape vines climbing high in the forest canopy can also be cut in the spring to provide copious amounts of mineral-laden water.

CHAPTER FIVE

Mountains, Plains, and Deserts

This section identifies a few of the more common edible wild plants found in unique environments. Each geographic location in the United States and Canada has endemic plant life that may not be found elsewhere. When traveling in mountains, deserts, and plains, it's a good idea to pack along an edible plants book for that specific locale.

JUNIPER (*Juniperus communis*)

Description. Prostrate and broadly spreading evergreen shrub about 3 feet high and may exceed 9 feet in circumference. Reddish brown, shredding bark; stiff, pointed, and prickly needles, whitish underneath and dark green on top: female cones look like blue black berries when mature, mature in second season.

Location. Found from East to West Coast, in the dry dunes area and dry open forests of the Midwest, throughout the mountain states, and north to the Arctic tundra.

WARNING. *Use sparingly, allergic reaction possible. Pregnant women should avoid this herb because it may induce uterine contractions. Do not eat if you* *may have kidney infection or kidney disease. May increase or induce menstrual bleeding. Use only under the care of a licensed holistic health care practitioner.*

Cooking tips. Use fresh crushed or dried grated berries in stews and to flavor wild game and domestic fowl. Berries may be made into tea; crush berry first and use judiciously, start with a half teaspoon of berries to a cup of green tea. Juniper berries may be infused into vodka and gin as a flavoring, try ten berries to a quart, add more for a stronger flavoring. Add berries to marinades of rosemary, oregano, ginger, and soy sauce. Grate dried berries on cold cuts. Try it on vegetated protein cold cuts like Wham and Mock chicken and soy burgers. Several varieties of schnapps and aquavit are flavored with juniper berries.

Medicinal uses. Extract is in the diuretic Odrinil. Also considered antiseptic and a digestive aid. Used traditionally in decoction to treat arthritis, rheumatism, and urinary tract problems. Contraindicated for kidney disease. Native Americans used juniper branches around tepees and shelters to fend off rattlesnakes. It is used in Europe to treat arthritis and gout. The diluted essential oil has been applied to the skin to draw and cleanse deeper skin tissue. Has been used to promote menstruation— see your holistic health care practitioner before treating dysmenorrhea.

SEGO LILY
(*Calochortus nuttalii*)

Description. Eight to 20 inches tall, erect, with unbranched stems; leaves lance shaped and basal, smaller clasping leaves on stem; flowers 1 to 3 inches across. Blooms June to July.

Location. On well drained to dry ground: plains, sage highlands, and high meadows, cliff sides, edges of washes (look around Devil's Canyon Ranch, Wyoming). Mountain states of the West (elevations from 5,000 to 9,000 feet) and the plains of eastern Montana and western North Dakota, south to Idaho and Nebraska.

Cooking tips. Bulbous root may be eaten raw or steamed; cook like a potato. Dried bulbs may be ground into flour for pancakes or corncakes. Sliced bulb used in Tortilla Espanola (see appendix 1) as a substitute for potatoes or Jerusalem artichokes. Good in potato soups. Roots may be boiled in sugar (hypertonic solution) and candied.

Medicinal use. Not specified in the literature or by personal experience. Raw root contains polysaccharides and may stimulate the immune system when eaten (unproven).

JOJOBA
(*Simmondsia californica*)

Description. Shrub. Seed capsules burst in early fall, disgorging oily, chocolate-colored edible seeds.

Location. Mountainous West, primarily the Sierras, and mountain borders into desert southern California.

Cooking tips. Seeds are eaten raw or cooked. Roasted and ground seeds are whipped in cooked egg yolks until paste forms. Boil in milk, sugar, and a little water. Add a drop or two of vanilla extract to flavor. Drink hot.

Medicinal uses. Native Americans used oil for growing hair and treating cancer and kidney problems. Oil has been applied to body and head sores and is reported to be emetic.

MINER'S LETTUCE
(*Claytonia perfoliata*)

Description. Leaves form cup or saucer around stems; delicate, small white flowers. Found in moist, shady places. High in vitamin A.

Location. Pacific coastal range, east to plains.

Cooking tips. Cook like dandelion greens or eat leaves and stems raw. Best with vinegar-laced salad dressing.

INDIAN BREADROOT, PRAIRIE TURNIP (*Psoralea esculenta*)

Description. Low-lying, hairy herbs of the prairie. Long-stemmed leaves, compound, divided into five fingers; flowers in dense, blue spike (each floret looks like small pea blossom). Edible part is 1- to 2-inch tuberous root.

Location. Prairie.

Cooking tips. Eat raw, sliced in salad with vinegar and oil dressing. Roots can be dried and preserved. Add dried root to soups and stews.

Medicinal uses. High in starch (may be 70 percent starch). *Psoralea* genus used to treat psoriasis and some forms of cancer (psoralen/photophoresis).

PRICKLY PEAR, INDIAN FIG (*Opuntia* spp.)

Description. Desert and prairie cactus. Spreads along ground on dry land in sandy soil. Broad but thin, spined, fleshy, pear-shaped but flattened segments; fruit pear shaped, rounded; yellow flower blooms in March and April.

Location. Desert.

WARNING. *Although I have eaten the flowers of several species of prickly pear and I have seen Mexicans eat the flowers in Del Rio, Texas, I cannot find any documentation on their safety. Until I discover whether or not prickly pear flowers can be eaten as food, I do not recommend them as food.*

Cooking tips. Harvest carefully, wear gloves. Peel or flame away spines. Slice "leaf" into segments and stir-fry, deep-fry, or roast over an open fire. Pulp of ripe fruit can be removed and made into jelly. I have eaten the flowers.

Medicinal uses. Leaf pad, split in half, makes an excellent compress over wounds.

Native Americans in the southwestern desert areas use a prickly pear compress over snake, scorpion, and spider bites.

P. pubescens

MESQUITE (*Prosopis juliflora, P. pubescens*)

Description. Woody tree or shrub of arid regions. Compound, featherlike leaves; seed pods resemble green bean pods.

Location. Desert.

WARNING. *May cause dermatitis.*

Cooking tips. Wood used to cook and flavor meats. Seed pods edible, juicy, sweet when ripe, very seedy.

Medicinal use. Native Americans of the Southwest treat adult-onset diabetes by including mesquite pods, beans, and prickly pear in their traditional diet.

AGAVE, CENTURY PLANT, MESCAL (*Agave* spp.)

Description. Long swordlike, stiff, fibrous leaves shooting skyward in circular cluster; 10- to 15-foot flower stalk grows from leaf cradle; clusters of yellow flowers.

Location. Desert.

Cooking tips. Young bud of plant can be cut out. Cut entire bud from leaves as it emerges. Trim away leaves and flower tips. Prepare fire in large pit lined with stones. Let large fire burn down to coals, then put bud in ashes. Cover bud with hot stones and ashes, and bury in dirt. Open the pit and recover

the cooked bud ten to twelve hours later. Cut away charred covering to expose sticky, sweet, pineapple-tasting interior. *Note:* You may need help from the local Native population to prepare the plant correctly.

Medicinal uses. Plant fruit is made into Native drink, mescal. Agave sap was used to seal and heal an ax wound in conquistador Cortez's thigh.

CHAPTER SIX

Seashore Tidal Areas

Almost all marine seaweeds are safe to consume, and the two questionable varieties are easy to avoid: foul-tasting *Lyngbya,* a thin, hairlike species that clings to mangrove roots in warm waters; and *Desmarestia,* which is found in deep, open waters and contains sulphuric acid and imparts an unpleasant lemonlike taste. Therefore, avoid mangrove-clinging seaweeds and deep open-water varieties.

Because of limited space only a few popular edible seaweeds are covered—by no means the limit of your foraging choices.

SEA ASPARAGUS, AMERICAN GLASSWORT, SALTWORT (*Salicornia virginica*)
SLENDER GRASSWORT (*S. maritima*)

Description. Fleshy mats. Individual plants grow from slender rhizomes; leaves are absent, reduced to tiny opposite scales; leafless stems are prostrate or erect, many jointed, with numerous flowering stems growing upright from the main stem; plant stems generally brown purple. Eastern variety is emerald green in spring to red in late summer.

Sea asparagus

Location. Coastal areas, beaches, salt marshes in the upper tidal zone from Washington state north in the West and Nova Scotia south in the East.

Cooking tips. Wash and eat stems raw or cooked—salty. Eat like asparagus. Boil, sauté, or fry young stems. Older stems are not tender. Fresh plant can be purchased in seafood and grocery stores on the Washington and British Columbia coast. Native Americans dried and ground the plant and used it like flour in cakes and bread, typically sweetened with honey. Stems are still eaten as food by Salish, Heiltsuk, and Goshute peoples.

Medicinal uses. External use (whole aerial parts of plants) by Heiltsuk peoples to treat edema, pain, arthritis, and rheumatism.

KELP (*Laminaria* spp.)

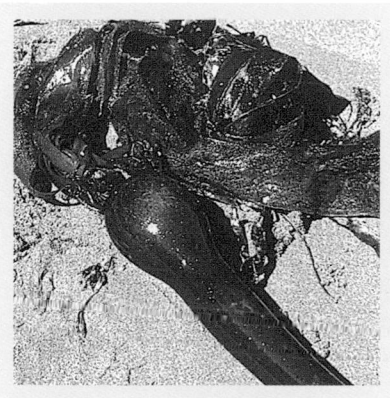

Description. A brown seaweed that can grow to more than 100 feet in length. Large frondlike leaves; stem can be thick as a human's wrist; air-filled bulbs or bladders hold plant erect in water. Plant is often torn loose and washed ashore after storms. *Note:* Gardeners are encouraged to spread seaweeds of all types on their organic gardens. Containing more than 90 minerals, marine algae are a wonderful addition to the garden. Excellent for fiber. Contain most minerals humans need.

Location. Found along the West Coast, from California to Alaska.

Cooking tips. Wash the plant in clean water. Soak in weak wine vinegar or lemon juice until pliable. Air-dry in sun. After drying, scrape off blue green surface layer. Thick white core can be chopped, shredded, or ground. Best cooked in soups and stews. Dry the shredded parts for later use. I have dried various seaweeds by spreading them on my car windshield in full sunlight.

Medicinal uses. Improves yolk color when fed to chickens. Good source of iodine (important clotting agent). Kelp salt prevents muscle cramps.

NORI, LAVER, PORPHYRA (*Porphyra* spp.)

Description. Rose pink to red brown with aging; flat, bladelike, irregular shape to

20 inches; satin sheen, thin, elastic. Nearly 36 percent protein. High in iodine and vitamins A and C.

Location. Mid-tidal zone.

Cooking tips. Forage in late spring. Sundry, then store in airtight canning jars or plastic bags. Use it fresh, seasoned, and tenderized in soy sauce. Dry and flake into baked goods or use in soups and stews.

Medicinal use. May lower blood cholesterol levels (as yet unproven).

ALARIA, WAKAME (*Alaria marginata*)

Description. Grows to 6 feet tall; olive brown to green; attached by short stem (stipe) and holdfast cell; short paddlelike sporophylls just below edible frond blades. Do not cut away sporophylls when harvesting—this procedure guarantees the life and future of your alaria supply. High in essential trace elements. Good source of pantothenic acid and vitamin C and B vitamins.

Location. Found on rocks in lower tidal zones.

Cooking tips. Dry plant. Can be restored with water to near-fresh condition. Wrap reconstituted alaria leaves around rice and meats, cook in casseroles, or simmer in pot roast. Great in mushroom soup. Especially good when used in chicken soups and stews.

NARROW-LEAFED SEASIDE PLANTAIN, GOOSE TONGUE (*Plantago maritima*)

Description. Long, narrow, lance-shaped leaves growing from basal whorl; no basal sheath; leaves with thick longitudinal ribs. Appearance similar to narrow-leafed garden plantain *(P. lanceolata).*

Location. West Coast of North America.

WARNING. *Goose tongue can be confused with arrow grass. Arrow grass leaves are flat on one side and round on the other, with sheaves at the base of the leaves. Goose tongue leaves have prominent ribs and are more flattened. If you cut the goose tongue leaf in cross section, it would appear flat or slightly V-shaped. The characteristic plantain spike of goose tongue is distinctive. Remember Wild Plant Foraging Rule #1: Follow these two plants through an entire season before eating goose tongue.*

Cooking tips. Succulently salty and mineral rich. Eat it fresh and raw. Can also be used as a stuffing for salmon. Mix it with finely sliced kelp and sauté it with olive oil and water. Then stuff the mixture in the cavity of a cleaned and washed salmon and steam the fish in a reed basket or in a Chinese basket steamer over a pot of boiling water until done.

Medicinal uses. Fresh leaves and fresh juice considered anti-inflammatory and antimicrobial. Native American healer Patsy Clark chews the leaves and applies them over wounds. In Germany the leaves are simmered in honey for 20 minutes to treat gastric ulcers.

BEACH PEA (*Lathyrus japonicus* var. *maritimus*)

Description. Marine coastal dweller that dawdles along upper littoral area of the beach. Beach pea leaves are compound, even numbered, typically six to twelve leaflets; leaflets tipped with a curling tendril typical of pea family; opposite leaflets about 2½ inches long. Fruit is pea pod–like and hairy about 2½ inches long.

Location. Coastal areas of East and West Coasts. Found in sandy upper areas of beach among driftwood and dunes.

WARNING. *Many members of the pea family are potentially toxic. Make positive identification, eat only small amounts of edible wild foods, and follow all foraging rules*

Cooking tips. Cook beach pea seeds in seal oil. If that's not practical cook them with salmon. New growth (stalks of spring) may be stir-fried, boiled, or steamed and eaten. After peas flower, tender young pods may be cooked and eaten like snow peas. The Inuits dried peas and roasted them like coffee then percolated.

Medicinal uses. The Chinese used peas as tonic for the urinary organs and intestinal tract. Eskimo considered the peas poisonous. Coastal Iroquois treated rheumatism with cooked whole young plant.

Appendix 1
Tapas-style Wild Plant Recipes

Friends and family may refuse to eat edible wild plant foods. Overcome this trepidation by combining edible wild plants in familiar dishes. Combining wild foods in everyday recipes broadens the palate and eases the novice into the experience. Here are a few combination recipes. Serve them as entrees or as Spanish tapas sampler plates.

The recipes are proven and delicious and were tested on more than 300 of my students, so you may use them with confidence. They are excellent examples of how edible wild plants can be substituted for traditional ingredients in a wide variety of recipes.

WILD GREENS SALAD

Add wild greens to head lettuce and mesclun mix. Strip dandelion leaves away from the tough mid-vein of the leaf. Tear the pieces smaller. Do the same with plantain. Add leaves of sheep sorrel and garden sorrel. Throw in some tender lamb's-quarters leaves. Mix in some purslane and bits of blanched wild asparagus. Amaranth leaves, too. Watercress? Sure. Now pick some violet flowers and a few violet leaves and throw them on. Very small amounts of fresh rosemary, basil, fennel, lovage, and French sorrel will balance the flavors. Add all these herbs and wild greens to the traditional salad and you have a powerful health-protecting starter. Powerful but not overpowering.

WATERCRESS AND LIME SALAD DRESSING

Makes 1½ cups

½ cup chopped watercress leaves

¼ cup chopped wild leeks, or
  substitute 1/2 cup
chopped green onions or scallions

juice of half a lime

1 tablespoon Dijon mustard

¾ cup light olive oil, or
  substitute vegetable oil

½ teaspoon each salt and pepper

1 egg yolk, beaten

Puree all the ingredients except the egg yolk. Then, with the blender running, drizzle in the egg yolk. Serve fresh. Shake or whisk before using.

WATERCRESS AND WILD LEEKS DRESSING (NO EGG YOLK)

Makes 2 cups

1 cup chopped watercress

2 wild leeks, chopped

2 tablespoons chicken broth
  (used instead of egg yolk)

1 teaspoon lemon juice

1 tablespoon white wine

1 tablespoon hot water

Salt and pepper to taste

Blend all until smooth. Whisk before using. Add a teaspoon of grated lime or lemon zest to achieve perfection.

WATERCRESS AND WILD LEEKS STIR-FRY

Serves 2, or makes 6 appetizer-size tapas dishes

3 tablespoons low-salt soy sauce

4 tablespoons stock (made of 1
  tablespoon seasoned rice wine
  vinegar and 3 tablespoons
  vegetarian stock)

2 tablespoons chopped ginger

½ teaspoon brown sugar (optional)

2 tablespoons peanut oil

6 whole wild leeks, cut lengthwise
  (i.e., cut bulb in half)

4 cups watercress (cut away large
  stems and chop coarsely)

1 teaspoon dark sesame oil

2 teaspoons toasted sesame seeds

3 tablespoons chopped cilantro

Combine soy sauce, stock, ginger, brown sugar, and peanut oil,. Swirl until hot in a wok or 12-inch frying pan. Add leeks, fry until tender (2 minutes). Add chopped watercress and cook for 1 more minute. Stir in sesame oil. Serve garnished with toasted sesame seeds and cilantro.

Options: Add or substitute chopped stinging nettle and chopped cattail shoots.

WILD MUSHROOMS WITH WILD LEEKS AND STINGING NETTLES

Serves 2, or makes 6 tapas

3 wild leeks, leaf and bulb chopped

1 tablespoon olive oil or enough canola spray to coat pan

6 chopped spring morels

4 cups chopped stinging nettle

2 tablespoons water

3 tablespoons walnuts, chopped and roasted

Salt and pepper to taste

3 tablespoons olive oil and 1 tablespoon aged red wine vinegar, combined as dressing

Sauté chopped leeks in olive oil for 1 minute, add chopped morels and stinging nettle and water, then stir-fry for 2 minutes until steam wilts the stinging nettle. Serve hot or cold with toasted almonds and olive oil and vinegar dressing.

Options: Add watercress to this recipe, also try with cattail shoots. Adding thin slices of burdock root is another option.

TORTILLA ESPAÑOLA WITH MORELS, WILD LEEK LEAVES, JERUSALEM ARTICHOKES, AND WILD ASPARAGUS

Serves 6, or makes 12 tapas

3 Jerusalem artichokes, sliced ¼ inch thick (enough slices to cover the bottom of a 10-inch iron skillet)

12 tender wild asparagus shoots

1 cup sliced and roasted green, yellow, or red bell pepper (combine or your choice)

1½ cups morel mushrooms, sliced, or substitute available edible mushrooms

1 cup cleaned and coarsely chopped watercress

1 cup chopped wild leek leaves

6 whole eggs

3 tablespoons fresh chopped cilantro

1 tablespoon Lawry's salt or equivalent, or substitute 1 tablespoon salt and 1 tablespoon pepper

¼ cup Parmesan cheese

Optional: 1 cup thinly sliced burdock root, or in the fall of the year use sliced ground-nuts and nettle, lamb's-quarters, and dandelion leaves

Preheat oven to 350°F. Spray bottom of iron skillet with nonstick oil. Arrange slices of Jerusalem artichokes across the bottom of the pan to form a base. Place asparagus shoots on top of the artichokes like the spokes of a wheel. Spread roasted peppers, mushrooms, and watercress over the first two layers, and sprinkle on some uncooked wild leek leaves.

Whip eggs, chopped cilantro, and salt and/or pepper, until frothy. Slowly pour the airy mix of eggs over the layers of vegetables in the skillet. Sprinkle top liberally with Parmesan cheese. Cook for 15 minutes in the heated oven, then brown the top for about a minute under the broiler. Cut like a quiche and serve over a corn tortilla with fresh salsa (see below) and refried beans.

RED SALSA WITH WILD LEEKS

Combine 1 cup chopped fresh tomatoes, 1 cup chopped onions, and half a jalapeño pepper, minced. Add the juice of half a lime, 3 minced wild leek bulbs, and 1 tablespoon chopped cilantro. Salt and pepper to taste. Makes 2 cups.

GREEN SALSA WITH WILD LEEKS

Boil 6 whole tomatillas until tender, about 5 minutes in water at a boil. Cool tomatillas in ice water. In an electric blender, combine tomatillas with 5 wild leeks, including leek bulbs and chopped leaves. Add ½ teaspoon of fresh or pickled jalapeño pepper, minced (optional); the juice of a quarter of a lime; and 1 tablespoon chopped cilantro. Salt and pepper to taste. Makes 1½ to 2 cups.

DIVORCED EGGS WITH MORELS AND WILD LEEK LEAVES

Serves 1

Red sauce represents anger and green sauce is for naivete, the colors of a failed marriage. This is a traditional Yucatecan breakfast.

2 tablespoons wild leek leaves, finely chopped

1 morel chopped

1 tablespoon butter

4 tablespoons green salsa

4 tablespoons red salsa

2 eggs

Salt and pepper to taste

1 teaspoon chopped cilantro

½ cup refried black beans

Sauté leeks and morel pieces in butter for 2 minutes. Warm the two salsas in the microwave separately (do not mix). Divide the chopped leek and morel mixture in half and add to salsas in equal amounts. Cook two eggs over easy. Pour green salsa over one egg and red salsa over other. Serve over oil-fried corn tortilla and garnish with cilantro and a side of refried beans.

VEGETARIAN WILD GREENS IN SPRING STOCK

Serves 6

1 cup chopped watercress

1 cup chopped wild leeks

1 cup chopped stinging nettle

1 cup chopped violet leaves

½ cup chopped dandelion leaves

1 cup chopped young (3-inch-high) daylily shoots

2 quarts chicken broth

Add coarsely chopped greens to a saucepan with 2 quarts of chicken broth. Bring to a boil, back off to a simmer for 15 minutes. Strain off broth and use for soup.

WILD PLANTS AND MOREL VEGETARIAN LASAGNA

Serves 4

Cheeses: ½ cup cottage cheese, ½ cup Parmesan cheese, and ½ cup ricotta

1 cup milk

1 egg

½ teaspoon each dried parsley, thyme, chervil, oregano, basil

½ cup chopped wild leeks

1 14- to 16-ounce can tomato sauce

3 cloves garlic, chopped

½ pound lasagna noodles

8 coarsely chopped morel mushrooms

2 cups chopped stinging nettle

1 cup finely chopped wild asparagus (domestic variety is okay)

¼ cup fresh basil

¼ cup fresh Italian parsley, chopped

Combine cheeses, milk, and egg. In a separate bowl combine dry seasonings, chopped leeks, and finely chopped garlic with the tomato sauce. Spread a thin layer of sauce on the bottom of a baking dish. Place a layer of *uncooked* dried lasagna noodles over the sauce. Ladle tomato sauce over lasagna noodles. Sprinkle mushrooms, nettles, and asparagus over sauce. Ladle a layer of cheese mixture over the vegetables. Add another layer of pasta, then repeat the sauce, vegetables, and cheese layers. Next, another layer of noodles, sauce, vegetables, cheeses. Top lasagna with a sprinkle of Parmesan cheese.

Bake covered in a preheated 325°F oven for 45 minutes. Cool. Garnish with chopped Italian parsley and fresh basil.

WILD LEEKS SALAD WITH ANCHOVIES IN VINAIGRETTE

Serves 6 to 8

1 quart water

30 wild leeks

3 eggs, hard boiled

5 anchovies, soaked several times in fresh water to release salt

To make vinaigrette:

Juice of 1 lemon

1 teaspoon chopped wild onion tops or, preferably, chives

Salt and pepper to taste

4 tablespoons olive oil

1 tablespoon finely chopped lovage, or substitute 3 tablespoons chopped parsley

Bring water to boil, add leeks, and simmer for 20 minutes. Cool leeks, dry, and refrigerate for 30 minutes. Combine vinaigrette ingredients. Peel and chop eggs coarsely and cut the anchovies into small bits. Spread cold leeks on a plate. Add chopped eggs and anchovies, drizzle all with vinaigrette, and garnish with lovage or optional parsley.

VEGETARIAN EGG ROLLS WITH WILD BERRIES AND MAPLE SYRUP SALSA

Serves 12

3 tablespoons maple syrup

¼ cup Reisling wine

½ cup blueberries, raspberries, blackberries, and autumn olive in combination or by themselves, or substitute any other wild berry

¼ cup dried elderberries

1 tablespoon soy sauce

2 tablespoons lemon juice

1 tablespoon Dijon mustard

1 tablespoon sesame seed oil

12 prepared vegetarian egg rolls or pot stickers

Mix maple syrup, wine, berries, soy sauce, lemon juice, and Dijon mustard. Bring to a boil and simmer and reduce until thick. Stir sesame seed oil into finished salsa. Steam pot stickers and/or egg rolls. Use salsa as dip or drizzle over pot stickers and egg rolls.

Note: When using autumn olive, it is necessary to press the berry juice through a sieve before serving to remove seeds.

NAVAJO FRY BREAD WITH AMARANTH SEED AND CATTAIL POLLEN

Serves 6

This is a 2:1 mix, 2 parts flour to 1 part skim milk. In the Paleolithic tradition I increase the fiber and protein in the dish by using whole grain flour such as buckwheat, oat, or whole wheat.

Grind ½ cup seven- or twelve-grain cereal in a mill, then mix with ½ cup whole wheat flour. Stir in ½ cup skim milk. Add 1 tablespoon sugar or ½ teaspoon Stevia (plant-based sugar substitute). Knead dough over a board sprinkled with flour, folding twenty or so times to form a moist, firm dough ball. Pluck an egg-sized ball from the dough, then roll it out flat on a floured board with a rolling pin until it forms a flat ⅛-inch pancake of dough. Cut a slit or two into the fry bread dough. In an 8-inch frying pan, heat 1 inch of canola or peanut oil to 400°F. Place the pancake (fry bread dough) into the hot oil and fry 5 or 6 seconds on each side (watch for the dough to fill with air and brown slightly).

Serve with autumn olive jam or huckleberry jam. Also good with black bean soup or refried beans.

COLD INFUSION OF MINT TEA

Serves 8

You will need something for your guests to drink while enjoying their edible wild plants repast. Try a cold infusion of wild mints. Cold infusions capture the essential oils and volatile compounds that are often lost in hot infusions.

In a gallon glass jar, combine equal amounts of peppermint, spearmint, mountain mint, lemon balm, and bee balm flowers *(Monarda didyma)* with juice of a lemon or lime. Cover with water and steep in the refrigerator for 10 hours. Simple and delicious.

Note: Fill the jar with all or any available combination of these mints

MISO BURDOCK SOUP WITH DAYLILY FLOWER GARNISH

Makes 2 cups

1 vegetable bouillon cube

1 cup water, or substitute vegetable stock

1 tablespoon miso soup base

1 burdock root

1 cup watercress

1 teaspoon sour cream

6 daylily blossoms

1 fennel leaf

Prepare this soup according to your taste for miso. I like using the lighter mix, the white miso: about a tablespoon to a cup. Peel and slice thinly (⅛ inch thick) the burdock root. Simmer the miso and burdock root for 10 minutes. Drop in a sprig or two of watercress for each cup. Simmer for 2 minutes more. Serve with a dollop of sour cream and garnish each bowl with 3 daylily petals and a feather of fennel leaf.

JERUSALEM ARTICHOKE SHOOTS AND STINGING NETTLE TEMPURA

Serves 4

This Japanese-style dish is simple to prepare and introduces friends to the pleasure of eating wild foods.

Break off early spring shoots of Jerusalem artichokes before the leaves open. Dip shoots in egg white, drop in bag of rice or wheat flour, shake, coat, and sauté or deep-fry until golden.

Pinch off the top whorl of leaves on stinging nettle, then batter dip and deep-fry, about 1 minute.

PAWPAW PUDDING

Serves 8

Here's a dessert to conclude the meal.

2 or 3 ripe pawpaws,
   enough to make 1 cup of puree

½ teaspoon baking soda

¼ pound unsalted butter, melted

1 cup sugar or substitute

   ½ teaspoon Stevia

2 eggs

1 tablespoon fresh lime or lemon

1 tablespoon dark rum

1 cup unbleached white flour

1 teaspoon cinnamon

½ teaspoon salt

1 cup chopped walnuts or butternuts

½ cup dried blueberries or
   raspberries or raisins

sour cream (optional)

Preheat oven to 325°F. In a mixing bowl, puree pawpaws with baking soda (the baking soda thickens the fruit). In a separate mixing bowl, blend melted butter, sugar, eggs, lime or lemon juice, and rum. Combine the remaining dry ingredients. Beat the two mixtures together. Stir in nuts and fruit.

Pour batter into greased cup Bundt or bread loaf pan. Set the pudding in a baking pan half filled with water. Cover the pudding with foil and bake for 2 hours or until it sets. Serve warm or chilled with a dollop of sour cream or heavy cream, if desired.

Appendix 2
Poisonous Plants and Poisonous Look-alikes

What follows is only a partial listing of poisonous plants in the United States. For a more comprehensive discussion, refer to the books listed in appendix 3: Recommended Books, Videos and Other Resources. Always keep the phone number of your poison control center in your wallet and your car.

AMERICAN LIVERWORT
(Hepatica americana)

Kidney- or liver-shaped leaves with hairy petioles; first flower of spring. Burning alkaloid, requires special preparation for consumption. Use reserved for skilled pharmacist or herbalist. See also page 42.

ARROW ARUM
(Peltandra virginica)

Arrow shaped leaf, pinnate veins; green primitive flower; grows in water. Some argue the burning alkaloids may be dried out of the seeds and roots. Even so, the bitter taste of the prepared plant is unfit to eat. All parts of this plant, including the flower and mature fruits, are poisonous.

BITTERSWEET, NIGHTSHADE
(Solanum dulcamara)

A climbing vine with purple rocket-shaped flowers, bearing a reddish orange fruit. Leaves lobed, alternate. Rarely fatal.

BLOODROOT
(Sanguinaria canadensis)

Plant's underground rhizome exudes a red "sap" when broken. Plant has a single, deeply dissected leaf; single white flower. Juice of plant is skin and eye irritant. Eating moderate quantities may be fatal.

BLUE FLAG AND OTHER IRISES
(Iris spp.)

Swordlike leaves; purple, blue, or yellow flower; rhizome. Causes diarrhea, vomiting, and dermatitis.

DATURA, JIMSONWEED
(Datura stramonium)

A large plant with spiny stems, spiny fruit pod, spined leaves, and spiny flowers. Hallucinations, delirium, and violent actions result from eating plant parts. Rarely fatal.

DEATH CAMAS, POISON SEGO
(Zigadenus spp.)

A sego lily look-alike. Eighteen inches high; grasslike; yellow or white flowers growing along central flower stalk. Has onionlike bulb but no onionlike odor. All parts toxic. May cause vomiting, headache, dizziness, and convulsions.

DUTCHMAN'S-BREECHES
(Dicentra cucullaria)

Deeply dissected, carrotlike leaves; white flower looks like "bloomers" or man's breeches. Tuber is poisonous. Causes convulsions and breathing difficulties, but is rarely fatal.

HELLEBORE, FALSE (Veratrum viride)

Large, ovate, stalkless leaves, clinging and spiraling up sturdy stem; flowers yellow green, in branched clusters. Grows in wet, swampy areas. Western variety of hellebore grows on open mountain slopes. May cause asphyxia, convulsions, and death.

HORSE NETTLE *(Solanum carolinense)*

Spiny stems and leaves. Leaves coarse, irregular, large toothed; white flower; fleshy, yellow berry fruit. Alkaloid, solanum. causes nausea, vomiting, and stomach and bowel pain.

JACK-IN-THE-PULPIT, INDIAN TURNIP *(Arisaema triphyllum)*

Flower has characteristic spathe and spadix like preacher in a pulpit. Calcium oxalate crystals burn when eaten fresh. See also page 44.

MAYAPPLE *(Podophyllum peltatum)*

A plant of the woods. Parasol-like leaf, deeply dissected; single white flower; yellow green fruit. Serious cases of plant ingestion may lead to coma and death. See also page 44.

MILKWEED *(Asclepias syriaca)*

Large ovate leaves; stomach-shaped fruit pod. plants exude milklike sap when damaged. Overdose of galitoxin (milk-wood toxin) has caused death in livestock. Eat shoots, flowers, and seed pods only with the guidance of an expert. Various species are more toxic than others. Proper cooking technique can destroy the potentially toxic cardiac glycosides. See also page 35.

POISON HEMLOCK *(Conium maculatum)*

Purple-spotted stems. Large plant, white flowers in many branched flower heads (umbels). Be careful, there are many edible look-alikes such as parsley, carrot, wild anise, parsnips and other members of the carrot family. Toxin, conine. Causes respiratory failure and death.

POISON IVY
(Toxicodendron radicans)

A climbing vine or shrub. Hairy stem; leaflets in threes; white or pale yellow berries. Contact may cause dermatitis. Jewelweed *(Impatiens capensis)* is a good treatment for poison ivy rash.

POISON OAK
(Toxicodendron diversiloba)

A small shrub. Resembles poison ivy (leaves more lobed). Contact causes dermatitis.

POISON SUMAC
(Rhus vernix)

Shrub with compound leaves; seven to fifteen leaflets; white fruits instead of red fruit of sumac. Causes dermatitis.

POKEWEED *(Phytolacca americana)*

Ovate leaves, pointed at tip; reddish purple stems; clusters of purple-colored fruit. Grows on wasteland. Rarely fatal, but can cause cramps and vomiting. See also page 25.

SKUNK CABBAGE
(Symplocarpus foetidus)

Wetlands dweller. Primitive fleshy plant; large ovate leaves; smells like skunk when torn or damaged; primitive flower (spadix and spathe). Terrible burning, bitter taste. Rarely fatal. See also page 42.

WATER HEMLOCK
(Cicuta maculata)

Inhabits wetlands. Has sharply toothed leaves, similar to poison hemlock in appearance. looks like many edible members of carrot family. *Beware:* Convulsions and death will occur a few hours after consumption.

Appendix 3
Recommended Videos, Books, and Other Resources

VIDEOS

Jim Meuninck has a free catalog of several one-hour videos and DVDs that identify and demonstrate the use of edible and medicinal wild plants. Call Jim Meuninck at (269) 699–7061, e-mail him at jim@herbvideos.com, or visit his Web site at www.herbvideos.com.

Cooking with Edible Flowers and Culinary Herbs, Jim Meuninck and Sinclair Philip (60 minutes/VHS, 1990).

Diet for Natural Health, Jim Meuninck, Candace Corson, M.D., and Nancy Behnke Strasser, R.D. (60 minutes/video with computer database, 1999). One diet for disease prevention and weight control.

Edible Wild Plants, Jim Meuninck and Dr. Jim Duke (DVD, 2006). One hundred useful wild herbs.

Herbal Odyssey, Jim Meuninck (CD ROM, 2005). Interactive media with World Wide Web linkages covering over 500 herbs, edible plants, edible flowers, and medicinal plants.

Little Medicine: The Wisdom to Avoid Big Medicine, Jim Meuninck and Theresa Barnes (DVD, 2005).

Native American Medicine, Jim Meuninck, Patsy Clark, and Theresa Barnes (DVD, 2005).

Natural Health with Medicine Herbs and Healing Foods, Jim Meuninck and Ed Smith, James Balch (60 minutes/VHS, 1992).

Trees, Shrubs, Nuts & Berries, Jim Meuninck and Dr. Jim Duke (60 minutes/VHS, 1990). Video field guide.

BOOKS

American Indian Medicine, Virgil Vogel (University of Oklahoma Press, 1970).

Edible Native Plants of the Rocky Mountains, Harold D. Harrington (University of New Mexico Press, 1967).

Edible Wild Fruits and Nuts of Canada, Nancy Turner and Adam Szczawinski (National Museum of Natural Sciences, 1979).

Edible Wild Plants, Oliver Medsger (Collier Books, 1966).

Field Guide to Edible Wild Plants, Bradford Angier (Stackpole Books, 1974).

Field Guide to Medicinal Plants and Herbs of Eastern and Central North America, 2nd ed., Steven Foster and James Duke (Houghton Mifflin, 2000).

Field Guide to North American Edible Wild Plants, Thomas Elias and Peter Dykeman (Van Nostrand Reinhold, 1982).

Handbook of Edible Weeds, James A. Duke (CRC Press, 2001).

Handbook of Medicinal Herbs, James A. Duke (CRC Press, 2001).

Handbook of Northeastern Indian Medicinal Plants, James A. Duke (Quarterman Publications, 1986).

Handbook of Nuts, James A. Duke (CRC Press, 2001).

An Instant Guide to Edible Plants, Pamela Forey and Cecilia Fitzsimons (Gramercy Books, 2001).

It's the Berries, Liz Anton and Beth Dooley (Storey Communications, 1988).

Medicinal and Other Uses of North American Plants, Charlotte Erichsen-Brown (Dover Publications, 1989).

Medicinal Plants of the Pacific West, Michael Moore (Red Crane Books, 1993).

Medicinal Wild Plants of the Prairie, Kelly Kindscher (University Press of Kansas, 1992).

Michigan Trees, rev. and updated, Burton Barnes and Warren Wagner Jr. (University of Michigan Press, 2004).

Plants of Coastal British Columbia, Jim Pojar and Andy MacKinnon (Lone Pine, 2004).

Sea Vegetables, Evelyn McConnaughey (Naturegraph Publishers, 1985).

Shellfish & Seaweed Harvests of Puget Sound, Daniel Cheney and Thomas Mumford Jr. (Puget Sound Books, 1986).

Sturtevant's Edible Plants of the World, U. P. Hedrick, ed. (Dover Books, 1972).

Traditional Plant Foods of Canadian Indigenous People, Harriet Kuhnlein and Nancy Turner (Macmillan, 1991).

Western Forests, Stephen Whitney (Alfred A. Knopf, 1985).

SEED AND PLANT RESOURCES

For catalogues and information on seeds and plants, contact the following:

American Botanical Council (512–926–4900; www.herbalgram.org). Ask for their book catalog.

Horizon Herbs (541–846–6704; www.horizonherbs.com). Rare wild plants, both edible and medicinal.

J.L. Hudson, Seedsman Catalog (www.jlhudsonseeds.net). Rare and unusual seeds.

Richter's Herb Catalogue (905–640–6677; www.richters.com). A free catalog of edible and medicinal plant seeds and live plants.

Seeds of Change (888–762–4240; www.seedsofchange.com). Free catalog.

Index

F

fiddlehead ferns *(Matteuccia* and *Pteretis* spp.), 46

G

garlic, wild *(Allium sativum)*, 34
gill-over-ground *(Glechoma hederacea)*, 24
ginger, wild *(Asarum canadense)*, 46
ginseng, American *(Panax quinque-folius)*, 52
glasswort, American. *See* sea asparagus
goat's-beard, yellow *(Tragopogon pratensis)*, 36
goose tongue. *See* seaside plantain, narrow-leafed
gooseberry *(Ribes* spp.), 15
grape, wild *(Vitis* spp.), 16
ground ivy. *See* gill-over-ground
ground-cherry *(Physalis pubescens, P. ixocarpa)*, 35
groundnut *(Apios americana)*, 53

H

hawthorn *(Crataegus* spp.), 29
hellebore, false *(Veratrum viride)*, 78
hepatica *(Hepatica americana)*, 42, 76
horse nettle *(Solanum carolinense)*, 78
huckleberry, evergreen *(Vaccinium ovatum)*, 11

I

Indian breadroot *(Psoralea esculenta)*, 62
Indian fig. *See* prickly pear
Indian potato *(Claytonia lanceolata)*, 51
Indian turnip. *See* jack-in-the-pulpit

J

jack-in-the-pulpit *(Arisaema triphyllum)*, 44, 78

Jerusalem artichoke *(Helianthus tuberosus)*, 30
jimsonweed. *See* datura
jojoba *(Simmondsia californica)*, 61
juniper *(Juniper communis)*, 59

K

kelp *(Laminaria* spp.), 65

L

lamb's-quarters *(Chenopodium album)*, 24
lantern plant. *See* ground-cherry
laver. *See* nori
leeks, wild. *See* ramps
liverwort, American. *See* hepatica

M

maple
 bigleaf *(Acer macrophyllum)*, 57
 red *(Acer rubrum)*, 56
 sugar *(Acer saccharum)*, 56
marsh marigold *(Caltha palustris)*, 43
mayapple *(Podophyllum peltatum)*, 44, 78
meadow salsify. *See* goat's-beard, yellow
mescal. *See* agave
mesquite *(Prosopis juliflora, P. pubescens)*, 63
milfoil. *See* yarrow
milkweed *(Asclepias syriaca)*, 35, 78
miner's lettuce *(Claytonia perfoliata)*, 61
morel mushroom
 black *(Morchella elata)*, 50
 yellow *(Morchella esculenta)*, 50
mountain ash *(Sorbus sitchensis, S. americana)*, 10
mountain potato *(Claytonia tuberosa)*, 51
mulberry *(Morus* spp.), 15
mullein, woolly *(Verbascum thapsus)*, 32

saltwort. *See* sea asparagus

sassafras *(Sassafras albidum)*, 54

sea asparagus *(Salicornia virginica)*, 64

seaside plantain, narrow-leafed *(Plantago maritima)*, 66

sego lily *(Calochortus nuttalii)*, 60

silverweed *(Potentilla anserina)*, 27

skunk cabbage *(Symplocarpus foetidus, Lysichitum americanum)*, 42, 79

slender grasswort *(Salicornia maritima)*, 64

sorrel

 garden. *See* sorrel, yellow

 sheep *(Rumex acetosella)*, 33

 yellow *(Oxalis stricta)*, 33

spatterdock. *See* pond lily, yellow

spicebush *(Lindera benzoin)*, 48

spiderwort *(Tradescantia virginiana)*, 37

spring beauty *(Claytonia caroliniana)*, 51

squaw vine. *See* partridgeberry

staghorn sumac *(Rhus typhina)*, 17

stinging nettle *(Urtica dioica)*, 32

strawberry *(Fragaria virginiana, F. vesca, F. californica)*, 12

sweet cicely *(Myrrhis odorata)*, 47

T

thimbleberry *(Rubus parviflorus)*, 19

trillium, white *(Trillium grandiflorum)*, 45

trout lily *(Erythronium americanum)*, 52

V

violets *(Viola* spp.), 22

W

wakame. *See* alaria

wapato. *See* arrowhead

water hemlock *(Cicuta maculata)*, 79

water lily, fragrant *(Nymphaea odorata)*, 6

watercress *(Nasturtium officinale)*, 2

willow

   black *(Salix nigra)*, 31

   weeping *(Salix alba)*, 31

wintergreen *(Gaultheria procumbens)*, 48

Y

yarrow *(Achillea millefolium)*, 39

About the Author

Jim Meuninck is a biologist and the author of two books and fourteen special-interest videos covering edible wild plants, edible flowers, medicinal herbs, natural health, survival, and other health and fitness topics.

He has lived and studied in four countries, documenting indigenous culture on four continents. His favorite pastime is discovering and preserving primitive technology. Jim has produced *Native American Medicine* and *Little Medicine*, DVDs exploring how First Peoples from Canada, Mexico, and the United States use plants in their spiritual life as food and medicine.

See Jim's Web site at www.herbvideos.com or e-mail him at jim@herbvideos.com.